To Bring Comfort and Consolation

Bereavement Ministry

Paddy Shannon
Foreword by Bishop Donal McKeown

\

Designed by Messenger Publications Design Department
Typeset in Times New Roman & Bembo
Printed by Hussar Books

Messenger Publications,
37 Leeson Place, Dublin D02 E5V0
www.messenger.ie

DEDICATION

This book is dedicated to the memory of my late parents,
Pat and Mary Shannon, and to my late brother and sister,
Frank Shannon and Mary (Shannon) Quigley.

So long thy power hath blest me, sure it still will lead me on,
O'er moor and fen, o'er crag and torrent, till the night is gone,
And with the morn those angel faces smile,
Which I have loved long since, and lost awhile.

(St John Henry Newman)

ACKNOWLEDGEMENTS

I would like to thank my wife, Ita, and my family for their forbearance while I have worked on this book. I am sure that, like myself, they wondered when it would ever be completed!

I also want to record my thanks to Dr Colin Murray Parkes for permission to quote freely from his work; Fr Brian D'Arcy for permission to quote from *A Little Bit of Healing*; Laurence McKeown for permission to quote his poem 'Solitary Man', from his book *Threads*; Fiona Brydon, Director of Communications, Cruse Bereavement Care, for permission to quote freely from *Bereavement Care* journal, published by Cruse.

I thank former clients/parishioners for entrusting their care to me and for giving me permission to use their suitably anonymised experiences.

Thanks too to Declan Smyth for the cover photograph and to Bishop Donal McKeown, Fr Jim Crudden and Patsy Curry for reading drafts and making some useful suggestions.

Finally, many thanks to the staff at Messenger Publications for their assistance and support in bringing this project to fruition.

∽ CONTENTS ∽

✂ FOREWORD ✂

Death is a reality of life. It can strike in all sorts of guises and at any age. Coming to terms with the prospect of death and the reality of bereavement is a huge challenge – and it takes time. So, it is not surprising that every culture has struggled with that unavoidable destiny of each human being.

Over the centuries the Christian tradition has developed a rich tradition of resources to help individuals and communities cope with the pain of loss. Familiar words and actions can go a long way to help when a loved one has been ripped out of their lives, often leaving a gaping wound.

On the one side, there is a wide range of teachings based on a belief in God and in the power of Jesus' resurrection. On the other side, there is a collection of culturally-sensitive rituals that support people of faith on the journey of loss and grief.

Many people struggle with how to process their reactions to the death of a loved one. In a culture where there is not a shared language about the meaning of life and death, we have seen the development of individual new secular rituals.

The Christian message offers a shared vocabulary and set of beliefs about the value of life and the questions raised by death. It does not merely offer vague spiritual words. It focuses on the painful encounter with personal loss, but puts it in a context of eternity.

This book comes from the author's extensive experience of ministry to the bereaved. It is grounded in having journeyed with people through the many stages of grief. Thus, we have a rich reflection on how bereavement can affect those who are left behind. The provision of scripture readings with associated reflections and sample intercessions can be enriching for the reader. And, ultimately, that can facilitate engagement between the gospel message and the unique reality of each person's pain.

Here we have a collection of scripture readings and other reflections that can be adopted and adapted for private, family and public use. They can provide material for a family or circle of friends to talk about their experience of loss – and for them to create an intimate, faith-centred liturgy that is sensitive to their situation. This could happen at the time of death or for other anniversaries.

A society that deals with death in a healthy way is a blessing on its members. I pray that this publication will be a blessing on many individuals, families and communities.

+Donal McKeown
Bishop of Derry

ᘓ INTRODUCTION ᘓ

Blessed be the God and Father of our Lord Jesus Christ,
the Father of mercies and the God of all consolation, who
consoles us in all our affliction, so that we may be
able to console those who are in any affliction with the
consolation with which we ourselves are consoled by God.
(2 Corinthians 1:3–4)

In 2012 I was invited by the parish pastoral council in Newcastle,
County Down, to help establish a bereavement ministry in the
parish.

The remit of those involved in this ministry to the bereaved is
to work alongside the priest in bringing comfort and consolation
to our grieving brothers and sisters in Christ and in commending
the deceased to the loving care of our heavenly Father. It is quite
fitting that all members of the Church exercise a responsibility
in the celebration of the funeral rites. The introduction to the
Order of Christian Funerals (Ordo Exsequiarum)[1] states that 'in
the celebration of a funeral all the members of the people of God
must remember that to each one a role and an office is entrusted'
(page x). It further states that whilst it is the norm for a priest or
deacon to conduct the funeral rites, 'As pastoral needs require, the
conference of bishops, with the Apostolic See's permission, may
even depute a layperson for this' (my emphasis) (ibid. page xi).

The order also outlines a duty to:

- To be at the side of the sick and the dying.
- To comfort the family of the deceased, to sustain them

---

1   All quotations and the pagination from the *Order for Christian Funerals* relate to the version
approved for use in Ireland, published by Veritas Publications in 1991. There is a separate version
approved for use in the Catholic Church in Scotland and in England & Wales (Liturgy Office,
England & Wales, 1988).

amid the anguish of their grief and to be as kind and as helpful as possible.

- To impart catechesis on the meaning of Christian death.
- To prepare with the family a liturgy for the dead that has meaning for them and to fit it into the liturgical life of the parish.

This latter point is becoming ever more necessary with the decreasing involvement of people in the life of the Church. For many today, their church attendance is confined to what is sometimes referred to as 'baptisms, brides and burials'. An effect of this is that when it comes to a family funeral, the bereaved relatives are often unsure about what to do, where to sit, when to stand, when to get up to read – in short, the responses and rubrics associated with church liturgies.

Those involved in bereavement ministry can assist families in the preparation of the funeral liturgy, not only in making it meaningful for them but also in making it a dignified service within the liturgical life of the parish.

TRAINING FOR THE BEREAVEMENT MINISTRY

As I set about preparing a training course for the ministry, I was unable to find exactly the course structure I was looking for in existing materials, and so I designed my own course.

OUTLINE OF THE COURSE

The course was delivered over ten modules covering the following areas:

- The context within which the bereavement ministry was being set up.
- Participants' own experiences of loss and grief.
- What some 'experts' have to say.
- Some particular issues, such as how children grieve, and

traumatic situations like bereavement by suicide.

- Learning about and practising some basic listening skills.
- What contribution does faith make to the grief story and what does it say in the scriptures and in the tradition of the Church?
- The liturgy of bereavement/mourning.
- The practicalities of how the ministry will be exercised.

This book captures much of the essence of the journey the trainees undertook. I have divided it into four chapters:

1. The Human Experience of Grief
2. The Liturgy of Mourning
3. Grief in the Scriptures
4. Suggested Readings, Reflections and Prayers

I have also included an appendix of prose extracts, poems and prayers that I have found inspirational and which I hope may also prove inspirational to readers.

What I have written is directed primarily to those involved in bereavement ministry. I offer my thinking and experience to support them in their work. I draw on the thoughts and experiences of those with whom I have had the privilege to work: colleagues, clients and parishioners. Whilst most of what I have written is from a Roman Catholic perspective, particularly the section on the Liturgy of Mourning, I hope that people of other faith communities will find my thoughts of some benefit.

CHAPTER 1

WHAT DOES GRIEF LOOK LIKE?

*Our new constitution is now established and has an appearance
that promises permanency; but in this world nothing can be said
to be certain, except death and taxes.*
Benjamin Franklin

Every one of us will experience loss and grief in our lives. Indeed, the very experience of being born involves an element of loss. Having spent forty weeks or so growing and developing in our mother's womb we are thrust from that dark, safe environment into the bright lights of the hospital delivery suite. Is it any wonder newborn babies cry! As life progresses we are faced with countless loss experiences, some not so significant, others hugely so. Some will be within the context of death whilst others will involve loss associated with life events like moving home, changing school or the death of a pet. Some losses will be the result of natural maturation; others may result from the experience of some traumatic event such as parental separation or death. Many of the reactions we have to these loss experiences will be very similar, varying only in duration and intensity.

Thanatology, the scientific study of death and grief, is a relatively recent phenomenon, and modern thinking on grief and bereavement has been greatly informed by the work of early pioneers in the field such as Sigmund Freud. It is impossible in a short work such as this to do justice to the complexities of Freud's contribution to the field, but it is fair to say that his thinking informed many of the studies that followed over the last century. In his seminal work, *Mourning and Melancholia* (1917), he applies his theory of explaining the psychopathological in terms of the normal, describing melancholia by comparing it with the normal experiences associated with mourning. He suggests that mourning reaches a conclusion when the grieving person is able to cut his/her emotional attachment to the lost one and reinvests his/her energies or drive in new objects, relationships or activities. This concept reappears in the writings of others through the intervening century to the present day. In his post-First World War writings, Freud identifies the process of melancholia as an integral component of mourning and in later writings raises the question of the endlessness of normal grieving. This is a question that is still at the heart of many contemporary discussions. How long does grief take? Will I ever get over it? That, of course, is an impossible question to answer. Some people will reach the point of being able to reinvest their energies within a couple of years, while some may never reach that point.

Following on from Freud's early work, others have presented various theories on the components of grief, stages of grief, phases of grief and tasks of grieving.

In November 1942 the Coconut Grove nightclub in Boston was the scene of the deadliest nightclub fire in history, killing 492 people. The enormity of the tragedy was such that it temporarily replaced the events of the Second World War in newspaper headlines. At the time Erich Lindemann was chief of psychiatry at Massachusetts General Hospital in Boston. He conducted a study of the survivors and in 1944 published a paper, *Symptomatology and Management of Acute Grief*, based on his work. His name has become synonymous with twentieth-century studies in the field of bereavement. He was the first to coin the term 'grief work', which was later taken up by other psychologists, including J. William Worden.

When I begin a bereavement training course I always ask participants to reflect on their own personal experience of loss, whether as result of bereavement or otherwise. I ask them to try to recollect what their reactions were in terms of feelings, thoughts, sensations and actions. I do this for several reasons. It helps them to realise that they know a lot about it already, and it demonstrates just how difficult it can be to express in words what it is that we are experiencing, which in turn makes our grief journey more difficult. As Shakespeare says in *Macbeth*, 'Give sorrow words; the grief that does not speak knits up the o'er wrought heart and bids it break.' When we do this exercise, I ask people to share in small groups of two or three and then write up with the whole group, what arises individually and collectively. Invariably what they come up with is consistent with what Erich Lindemann describes as the components of a normal grief reaction.

The reactions that we can expect to our experience of loss can be classified as emotional, physical, behavioural and spiritual. The lists that follow are by no means exhaustive but encapsulate much of what people recount from their experiences.

EMOTIONAL REACTIONS	PHYSICAL REACTIONS
Numbness	Muscle weakness
Yearning	Fatigue
Pining	Increased blood pressure
Guilt	Hypersensitivity, e.g. to noise
Hopelessness	Hyperactivity
Helplessness	Decrease in activity
Despair	Sleep disturbance
Anger	Increase in appetite
Bitterness	Decrease in appetite
Sadness	Neglect of self
Euphoria	Increase in self-care
Relief	Deep sighing
Feeling lost	Dry mouth
Peacefulness	Nausea

BEHAVIOURAL REACTIONS	SPIRITUAL REACTIONS
Searching	Searching
Social withdrawal	Loss of faith
Crying	Increase/renewal of faith
Preoccupation	Anger at God
Forgetfulness	Helplessness
Disorientation	Hopelessness
Lack of concentration	Confusion
Apathy	Insecurity
Seeking solitude	Fear
Seeking forgiveness	Sense of having been punished
Giving forgiveness	Guilt
Finishing 'unfinished business'	

In 1988 I worked at an International Conference on Grief and Bereavement in Contemporary Society, held at the Queen Elizabeth II Conference Centre in London. At the conference I was privileged to meet and listen to John Bowlby. Bowlby, who died in 1990, is widely known and internationally respected for his work on attachment theories, particularly his three-volume *Attachment and Loss*. Bowlby's work is believed to have been sparked by his own early life experiences. Born in 1907 to an English upper middle-class family, much of his early life was spent in the care of a nanny and he was sent off to boarding school at the age of seven, which he later described as a hugely traumatic experience. After serving with the Royal Army Medical Corps in the Second World War, Bowlby went on to work at the Tavistock Clinic in London where much of his pioneering work was done. Colin Murray Parkes worked at the Tavistock with Bowlby for thirteen years. I worked with Colin over some twenty years through my work with the organisation Cruse Bereavement Care of which he is Life-President. Parkes is a prolific writer, and one of his best-known works is *Bereavement: Studies of Grief in Adult Life*, first published in 1972 and revised and reprinted many times since. It has long been recognised as the most authoritative work of its kind. The notion of people typically going through phases of grief owes much to Bowlby and Parkes. The idea that there are four phases of grief is attributed to them.

✑ Phase I: Numbness

The news that someone we love has died is undoubtedly a mind-numbing experience. This is particularly true when the death is of a young person or is sudden and unexpected but can also be the case when it happens at the end of a prolonged illness. The deaths of both my parents occurred after illnesses and were expected. My mother died at the age of fifty-nine having had surgery and radiotherapy treatment for a brain tumour. My father died at the age of eighty-five from lung cancer. We had sat with both of them for weeks before they died and were well aware of the terminal nature of their illnesses. Nonetheless, at the moment of death there was still a sense of shock and numbness. That numbing of the senses experienced when a death occurs, even when expected, is often hard to put into words. In some ways I describe it as nature's anaesthetic. It enables us to cope with some of the practicalities that inevitably have to be faced. Indeed, sometimes people say how well the bereaved person coped, how strong they were, when often it was numbness rather than strength that saw them through. The numbness may well be interrupted by intense distress but can continue for weeks and even longer after the death.

✑ Phase II: Yearning and Searching

This phase of grief is characterised by the bereaved person pining for the one who has died; yearning for them to be back again. When any one of us loses something precious to us it is the most natural thing in the world to yearn for that thing and to search for it. We lose a purse, a wallet, car keys or a precious ring and what do we do? We search and search. We search in places where we have already searched. A friend told me once how he would have spotted women who reminded him of his dead mother, who looked like her, and followed them in the street before the realisation hit him that it wasn't her at all.

A whole variety of reactions can be experienced during this phase, e.g. anger, confusion, anxiety and crying.

℘ Phase III: Disorganisation and Despair

The numbness has worn off. The searching has failed to find. No matter how much I've pined, I haven't got my loved one back. Despair sets in. It is common in this phase for the bereaved person to withdraw from activities they normally engage in and to withdraw socially. Another feature of this phase can be weight loss as the person loses interest in eating. The converse is also true. The individual may gain weight through comfort eating.

As the pining and yearning become less intense so apathy and despair increase. It is in this phase that people can develop a clinical depression for which they require psychiatric intervention or treatment with anti-depressant medication. It is, however, important that we do not confuse this with the very natural 'downness' that we all experience at times of sorrow.

℘ Phase IV: Reorganisation and Recovery

In this fourth phase, thoughts of sadness and despair diminish, and people gradually experience an increase in energy levels and a desire to return to previously enjoyed activities. Sadness gives way to more positive thoughts and memories of the deceased.

It is in this phase that some writers describe the phenomenon of establishing a new identity. Our identity is closely linked to our relationships. When my wife and I got married she changed her surname to mine, thus having to get a new passport and new driving licence and to change her name with the tax office and other agencies. When my children came along, and I started going to parent/teacher meetings, I found that in those situations my identity was as parent. For example, teachers would address me as 'Sarah's dad'. That became my identity. In other circumstances people would say, 'Oh, you're Ita's husband'. So, in a sense I had a variety of identities, based on being a son, a husband, a parent, a friend or a work colleague. When a person with whom we are in relationship dies that particular identity changes or ends.

For some people this change in identity can be very challenging. For instance, when Prince Albert died Queen Victoria adopted the new identity of the widow. She dressed in black for the rest of her life and became known as the Widow of Windsor. As a child in Belfast in the late 1950s and early 1960s I remember older women in church wearing black shawls. I was to discover that these were widows. In days gone by it was commonplace for women not just to adopt their husband's surname on getting married, but also his forename, as in Mrs John Smith. If a woman was widowed, she would thereafter be addressed as Mrs Mary Smith. Another change of identity.

Thus the experience of establishing a new identity can be either positive or negative, depending very much on how we have progressed through the preceding phases. On the one hand, some bereaved people establish a new identity or role that is positive and constructive; on the other hand, there are those whose new identity becomes that of the widow or the bereaved person, much in the way a person with a particular health condition might adopt the identity of 'invalid'.

Whilst many people subscribed to the four-phase model of grief, a Swiss psychiatrist, Dr Elisabeth Kübler-Ross, posited a five-stage model of grief. This was based mainly on her work with terminally ill patients. She originally introduced the model in her 1969 book, *On Death and Dying*.

✐ Stage I: Denial

This stage is akin to the phase of numbness described in Phase I above. We deny the reality. In effect, we numb ourselves to what has happened. Life as we knew it, the reality within which we lived, has changed inexorably. We wish we'd wake up and discover this was all a bad dream. In a way, as with the numbness phase, this enables us to cope with many of the practicalities of the initial few days or weeks. It's our inner self saying, 'Hang on, there's only so much I can cope with just now.' In *A Grief Observed*, C. S. Lewis reflected that ' … it feels like being mildly drunk, or concussed. There is a sort of invisible blanket between the world and me. I find it hard to take in what anyone says. Or perhaps, want to take it in.'[2]

It's when this denial and shock begin to wear off that the reality intrudes and feelings that were suppressed break through, front and centre.

✐ Stage II: Anger

This is the stage of 'It's not fair', or 'Why me?' I remember when my mother died in 1982. It was a time of great turmoil in our part of Ireland. Murder and maiming were commonplace and yet, as I saw it, it wasn't the

2   C. S. Lewis, *A Grief Observed* (London: Faber & Faber, 1961).

murderers who were being 'punished'. Something bad has happened; we feel angry about it and we look for a target for that anger. I sometimes think about the story of the Fall in Genesis when God confronted Adam and Eve for eating from the tree of knowledge and expelled them from the Garden of Eden. Eve blamed the serpent; Adam blamed the woman – she tempted me, and I ate. He then blamed God – 'the woman you put with me'. And we have been doing just that ever since! When something bad has happened, we need a target for our anger and reach out to the nearest subject. It might be God, it might be other family members, it might be the doctors. It doesn't mean they are to blame; it is simply that we need someone to blame. Indeed, we might even blame the person who has died. This is particularly true when the death has been by suicide. 'Why did he do this?' 'Why did he choose death in preference to life with me?' It could be that we are angry that our loved ones didn't take better care of themselves. 'He should have gone to the doctor sooner.' 'He should have quit smoking.' 'He should have lost weight when he was told to.'

Sometimes the anger manifests itself as guilt. In some ways guilt and anger are either side of the same coin. We are angry, but flip the coin and we are directing the anger at ourselves. It might be that we are feeling guilty for feeling angry at the person who has died or even for feeling angry at all! Maybe it's feeling guilty about other feelings such as relief – relief that the dead person's suffering is over or that the weight of caring for them has been lifted from us. We sometimes feel guilty for not being stronger. Sometimes it is because we think we are acting contrary to our faith. This person has gone to heaven and so, surely, we should be happy for them and not indulging in selfish grief?

✑ Stage III: Bargaining

The shock and numbness are wearing off, letting the twin monsters of anger and guilt enter my broken world. If only they would pass. It's a bit like how the evangelist Matthew tells of Jesus praying in Gethsemane, 'If it is possible let this cup pass me by' (Matthew 36:29). And so, we bargain. This bargaining is very common in the case of someone diagnosed with a serious or terminal illness. 'God, if you heal me/my child/my partner, I'll be such a good person. I'll do X, Y or Z.' We try to negotiate ourselves out of our grief. When the bargaining doesn't work we can find ourselves in the middle of the anger and guilt again and moving into a stage of depression.

✑ Stage IV: Depression

This stage is much the same as the phase of despair and disorganisation described in the phases model above. It was the basis of Freud's *Mourning and Melancholia*. Typically, we find ourselves overwhelmed by the enormity of the prospect of facing the world and those in it; of meeting other people; of engaging in living; of starting back to work; of socialising. Some might even ponder on the question, 'Is life worth living at all?' This depression to the point of suicidal ideation is not to be confused with the 'downness' we can experience when confronted by loss and grief. Most of us in this stage of grief do not need treatment by a psychiatrist nor do we need anti-depressant medication. We may, however, benefit greatly from the services of a supportive listener or a counsellor.

✑ Stage V: Acceptance

The fifth and final stage of grief proposed by Kübler-Ross is acceptance. This stage resonates with the fourth phase in the phases model. We have arrived at a point where our emotions have begun to stabilise, and we realise we are going to be okay. We find times when we suddenly realise that we have gone perhaps most of the day without our thoughts being dominated by the person who died; days described by John O'Donohue as 'days when you wake up happy; Again inside the fulness of life … Days when you have your heart back, you are able to function well.'[3] The bad days outnumber the worse days and the good days outnumber the bad. We have accepted the reality that the deceased person is gone and is not coming back. We have adapted our lives to living in that new reality. We begin to socialise again. We begin to re-engage with friends. We may begin to form new relationships. Past hobbies once again hold an interest for us. Holidays are again an option for us. The night has gone, and the dawn is beginning to break; the rain has eased, and the rainbow adorns our sky.

A frequently asked question is, 'How long does it take to go through these phases or stages?' The simple answer is we can't put a time on it. It is as different for each person as each person is different from another. It is often said that time heals. My own view is that time of itself does not heal, but we can heal in time. In a way that can be a problem associated with the concept of a phase or stage process. People often mistakenly over-simplify the concept in that they expect that on day one they will begin at phase or stage one and progress through the rest until arriving at the end point. This is an over-simplification and not what was intended by those who formulated the concepts. I remember when I worked as a bereavement counsellor hoping that my client was not someone who had read a leaflet about phases or stages of grief. I invariably found such people coming to me saying that they had experienced say, stage one or two but had missed out on stage

3   John O'Donohue, 'For Grief', *Benedictus*, London: Bantam Press, 2007.

three. The reality is that people tend not to experience these stages or phases sequentially. Some people may never experience anger or guilt for example. They may experience several stages together or oscillate back and forth between two stages. The concepts do lend themselves somewhat to this form of misinterpretation.

I first met American psychologist J. William Worden in 1988 at a conference in London. Bill had developed the concept of *tasks* of mourning because he viewed the theory of phases or stages, whilst still being valid, as implying a degree of passivity; it is something that happens to us; we simply go through it. On the other hand, thinking in terms of tasks of mourning gives the bereaved person some semblance of control. There is something they can do to take charge of this process of mourning. They can take control, rather than being controlled. His theory sits well with me.

Worden proposes four tasks of mourning.

✍ Task I: Accept the Reality of the Loss

We live in a society that finds it difficult to talk about death – even to use words like 'death', 'dead', or 'died'. In earlier times death was less sanitised. More people died at home, extended families lived together or near each other and many of us encountered death at a young age. We grew up more comfortable talking about death. Today if you read the death notices in your local newspaper, you'd be astonished at how few people actually die! I recently looked through my daily newspaper and counted 147 obituary insertions in the Death Notices section. Of these only thirty-five referred to someone's death. Eleven 'passed' or 'passed away'; eight were 'called'; two 'fell asleep'. For fifteen there was just their name (presumably they had died), and for the remaining seventy-six it simply said 'peacefully at … '. Not using the words 'dead', 'death' or 'died' can be a symptom of not accepting the reality. There are myriad euphemisms that we use to avoid the stark finality resonating from those words. We use terms such as 'passed away', 'called home', 'gone to his reward', 'fallen asleep'. Or, in a less reverent attempt at black humour, we might use terms like 'shuffled off his mortal coil' or 'pushing up daisies'. This all resonates with Kübler-Ross's denial stage.

It is common for bereaved persons to keep the deceased's room as it always had been or to keep their clothes – almost saying they might be back. A more extreme example of this behaviour was how, after the death of Prince Albert, Queen Victoria had his clothes laid out for him each morning as well as his razor and shaving soap. She was frequently heard talking to him as she walked around Buckingham Palace. In Dickens's *Great Expectations*, Miss Havisham retained everything as it was when she was jilted by her bridegroom on the day of their wedding. She never removed her wedding dress and had the clocks in the house stopped at 08.40, the time she received the news of her fiancé's leaving her. She even left the wedding cake and wedding breakfast uneaten on the table.

It is in order to help people acknowledge the reality of a death that one of the first things I say to a bereaved client is, 'I am sorry to hear that your husband/wife/father/mother *died.*' 'Tell me about the *death.*' I very deliberately use the words 'died' and 'death' and encourage the bereaved person to do the same. When my sister died recently I encouraged the family, when preparing the obituary notice, to describe her as having died rather than as having 'passed away'.

∽ Task II: Work through the Pain of Grief

Worden says that the German word *schmerz* is a useful descriptor for the pain of grief because it encapsulates not just physical pain, but the sort of emotional pain or heartbreak associated with loss. The pain of grief is every bit as real as any physical pain. Some people try to avoid the pain by use of medication. Sadly, this is sometimes encouraged by medical practitioners. I remember visiting the home of a woman whose son had taken his own life. While I was with her, her GP arrived and after a few minutes' conversation he reached into the breast pocket of his jacket and brought out a prescription, already made out in her name, for Valium. I am sure he meant well, but I am not so sure that the woman needed drugs at that time. Drugs can have their place, but they need to be properly managed in order to avoid misuse or dependency. Other people try to avoid the pain through use of alcohol. Yet more will become 'workaholics'. This behaviour is partly a way of deflecting the enormous pain they know is there, but it can also be that they don't want to appear weak and unable to cope. The reality, of course, is that when the Valium wears off, when the person sobers up or sits back from the 'busyness', the pain is still there to be experienced and confronted.

I have arthritis in my neck and lower back. I can manage the pain through the use of some medication, but I will always have arthritis. I learn to live with it and control it rather than letting it control me. The bereaved person will always be bereaved but needs to acknowledge the pain and learn to control it rather than be controlled by it.

∽ Task III: Adjust to an Environment in which the Deceased is Missing

A former colleague, when giving a talk on grief, used to ask, 'What would I lose if my wife died?' He would then go through a list – best friend, lover, cook, childminder, fashion adviser and so on. What he was getting at was that he would be facing life without the person who provided for all these needs. He would have to adjust to a new environment. A friend once told me how, when her husband was diagnosed with a terminal cancer, he began to teach her some of the skills needed to fulfil many of the tasks around the home usually performed by him. He taught her how to set the central heating clock; how to change a wheel on the car; how to start the lawnmower; how to hang wallpaper. He knew that in his absence his wife would need to adjust to his not being there. The loss of a partner, parent, child or other significant person is not just the loss of the individual but has many associated secondary losses.

Of course it is not only on that kind of physically practical level of doing things that we lose out. A woman told me how after her husband died, she had nobody to argue with! In their relationship she had someone with whom she could safely disagree on things like politics. Now that her husband was gone, she had to 'bite her lip' a bit more often! There is also the question around the ability to make decisions. Many couples have harnessed the ability to arrive at joint decisions. It might be about seemingly trivial matters, such as what colour of paint to buy, or about more serious issues, such as how to invest their savings. Another client told me she found it really difficult to make the simplest of decisions. If her husband and she had been out shopping, she would show him some item and ask for his opinion. He would often just reply, 'Yeah, whatever you think', and she would go ahead and buy it. Although his input had been minimal she couldn't even decide on what to buy for dinner!

In the absence of the other person, we may also have to adjust our sense of direction in life. Some people talk about feeling 'rudderless' without the other person. Sometimes, for example, a brother or sister in a family can be the 'go-to person' when we feel lost or in need of direction or support. This third task can be about adjusting to the absence of that direction.

For some people the death brings with it a challenge to their faith or religious beliefs. Perhaps it is as simple as the fact that the one who died shared that faith and supported you in yours. The circumstances of the death can lead people to question their faith in a loving God who had been central to their life. Rather than being a comfort in their grief, their faith becomes another loss to adjust to. It may be a case not so much of finding an answer but of finding how to live life without one.

∽ Task IV: Emotionally Relocate the Deceased and Move on with Life

This task is, I believe, open to a number of interpretations or misinterpretations. It is for this reason that Worden himself has reworked/reworded it a couple of times. In his original presentation of it he described it as withdrawing emotional energy from the deceased and reinvesting it in another relationship. That, he now says, sounds too mechanical.

I like to think of it as almost a mixture of the two. I believe that when someone we love, and who loved us, dies we withdraw that love and energy back into ourselves again. To me this task is about accepting that while the person has died, the love hasn't died. In working on this fourth task we can emotionally relocate that love so that we are free to love others again. There is a sense in which we are still in a loving relationship with the one who has died, but it is not so much in a here and now physicality as in cherished memory. My mother died at a relatively young age a couple of years before I got married. I still love her deeply and I firmly believe that our love for each other still exists but on a different plane. I can also say that I loved my mother-in-law but that doesn't mean I loved my own mother any less. In the context of the fourth task, I believe it shows that I have emotionally relocated my mother and freed myself to reinvest in other relationships. In my view this is what Freud meant when he talked about reinvesting one's energies.

A problem with all these ways of understanding grief is the possibility of misinterpretation. In introducing the four tasks of mourning I referred to the expectation on the part of some people that they would somehow simply pass through the phases or stages and out the other end, even if this is not what those who formulated them intended. While Worden's tasks model seeks in part to address this, it too can be misinterpreted. There are some who read the tasks as something to be worked through in a linear, sequential way as some kind of continuum of grief work. This is of course not the case. People could be working on several tasks at once or go back and forward among them. Indeed, I would suggest that it wouldn't be healthy to focus, for example, on the second task exclusively for any length of time. It would be too emotionally painful and draining. Rather it would be better to go back and forth between it and, say, the third task of adjusting. Our psyche simply couldn't manage such exclusive focus on the pain of grief.

Margaret Stroebe and Henk Schut addressed this issue when they came up with a model of grief called the dual process model.

At the risk of over-simplifying it, the dual process model suggests that the grief process operates on two levels: loss-oriented and restoration-oriented. 'Loss-oriented' refers in essence to the more emotional aspects of the grieving process, whilst 'restoration-oriented' refers to some of the more practical aspects akin to elements of Worden's third task.

- **Loss-oriented responses** include many of the components of a normal grief reaction detailed earlier in this book, e.g. anger, guilt, despair, helplessness, hopelessness, sadness, fear, denial. They also include the embracing and verbalising of the pain of grief.

- **Restoration-oriented responses** include taking on roles and tasks previously done by the deceased, learning new skills, forming new relationships, similar to Worden's third and fourth tasks. They also include distraction from the acute pain associated with grief.
- **Healthy grieving** involves oscillating between the two aspects and is the way in which most people experience grieving, albeit not in a consciously decided way.

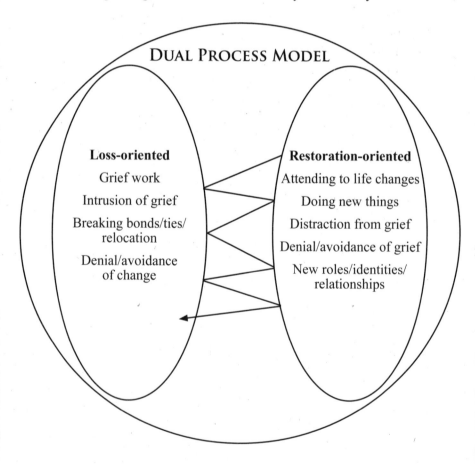

DUAL PROCESS MODEL

Loss-oriented

Grief work

Intrusion of grief

Breaking bonds/ties/
relocation

Denial/avoidance
of change

Restoration-oriented

Attending to life changes

Doing new things

Distraction from grief

Denial/avoidance of grief

New roles/identities/
relationships

So here we have a variety of theories on bereavement, grief and mourning. In my thinking bereavement is the state in which we find ourselves after the death of a loved one; grief encapsulates the myriad emotional and physical reactions we experience in that state; mourning is the process through which we work to make some sense of what has happened, to integrate it into our being and embrace the new reality in which we find ourselves.

Whichever model or combination of models we favour, one thing is sure – it is the way in which grief surprises us. In my own experience there have been times when I thought to myself – foolishly it seems – that I was through it. I was through the stages; I had completed the tasks, only to be ambushed by my grief again, as if from nowhere. I recall working with a physical health and disability social work team in Belfast and visiting a woman dying from cancer. She was near the end and she reminded me so much of my mother, so ravaged was she by this horrible disease. I remember leaving the house and crying in my car. It was ten years after my mother's death, and I was sure my grief was done and dusted. It was what the late John O'Donohue seems to me to be saying in his poem of blessing, 'For Grief':

> There are days when you wake up happy;
> Again inside the fullness of life,
> Until the moment breaks
> And you are thrown back
> Onto the black tide of loss.
>
> Days when you have your heart back,
> You are able to function well
> Until in the middle of work or encounter,
> Suddenly with no warning,
> You are ambushed by grief.[4]

4   O'Donohue, 'For Grief'.

As we begin our journey through grief, whether focusing on the early phases, addressing Kübler-Ross's first stage of denial or Worden's first task of accepting the reality, that first step can be the hardest. I believe that what is most important in that early time is to find the courage and strength to speak it out. As I said earlier in this work, Shakespeare puts it well in *Macbeth* (Act IV, Scene iii) when Malcolm says, 'Give sorrow words; the grief that does not speak knits up the o'erwrought heart and bids it break.'

In Ireland, this process traditionally begins within the context of the wake and the funeral. The wake is a time-honoured tradition whereby a vigil is kept in the few days between the death and the burial or cremation. It is a time when family and friends gather to remember the deceased, to share stories and memories of the person and comfort the bereaved. It can be a wonderful mixture of tears and laughter as tales of the deceased person are shared. It reminds me of what is described in Ecclesiastes as 'A time for tears, a time for laughter; a time for mourning; a time for dancing' (Ecclesiastes 3:4). For many this is a highly cathartic experience. Often the bereaved person gets to tell their story over and over again; telling how their loved one died; where they were at the time; how they heard the news. This is a great vehicle for grounding the death in reality. It is also an opportunity to hear how other people knew their loved one in other contexts, such as in the work setting or socially. I recall hearing Professor Tony Walter, author of *Funerals and How to Improve Them* (1990), talking about helping the bereaved person build a biography of the deceased. He or she meant different things to different people. For instance, people who worked with my father or who socialised with him over a game of cards knew a different aspect of him than I did. Even within families, siblings will have had different relationships with a deceased parent. They have lost the same person but have not lost the same things. Building that broader picture or, as Tony Walter described it, building a biography, can be really comforting.

Many non-Irish people that I have met have expressed a degree of envy for our Irish wake. Sadly, it is somewhat on the wane in modern Irish society, due partly I believe to the increasing growth of the funeral home culture with the body no longer reposing in the family home.

After the wake comes the funeral. For most people that takes the form of some kind of ritualised farewell or commendation. In my life experience, and in my belief and faith, that is the Requiem Mass and associated prayer services. This takes me to the next section of this book – what I choose to call the liturgy of mourning.

❦ CHAPTER 2 ❦

Liturgy of Mourning

As they celebrate the funerals of their brothers and sisters,
Christians should be intent on affirming their hope
for eternal life. (Order of Christian Funerals)

In the journal *Bereavement Care* (vol. 9, no. 2), the editor, introducing an article by the Anglican priest David Durston on the funeral service in the process of grieving, writes, 'There is no society known to anthropologists which does not carry out some formal ritual or rituals after death. These may be seen as a tribute or service to the dead but their importance to the survivors should not be underestimated.'[5]

The funeral service, be it religious or secular, is an important step in the grieving process. It can concretise the reality of the death and marks a farewell from this life to whatever lies on the 'other side'. For humanists there is no existence after death. For Christians and for people in other faith communities there is an afterlife, heaven, nirvana, svarga, call it what you will. The three great monotheistic religions, Judaism, Islam and Christianity all believe in life after death. In Hinduism and in Buddhism there is belief in *samsara*, a cycle of death and rebirth or reincarnation in which the *atman* (soul) is reborn into a new body and a new life. For Buddhists, escape from this cycle is described as nirvana or enlightenment.

---

5   *Bereavement Care*, vol. 9, no. 2, 1990, 18.

It is worth reflecting that in some particularly traumatic situations it is not possible to see the body of our loved one or, indeed, to hold a traditional funeral. In the course of my working life I have been present with people in these kinds of circumstances – after the 9/11 attacks in New York, a plane crash in England's East Midlands and, of course, in the aftermath of bombings and shootings in the North of Ireland. More recently the impact of the Covid-19 virus meant that families could not be with the dying person, could not see their body or kiss them goodbye, or in some cases not even be physically present at the funeral. When my sister was dying, Covid regulations meant that I was unable to see her, sit with her, hold her hand, pray with her or even kiss her goodbye. Some people were unable to perform the religious ritual washing of the body, traditional within their faith communities. This, undoubtedly, has a negative impact on bereaved people's mourning process.

Regardless of which religious practice or form of humanism or atheism we follow, the ritual farewell of the funeral rite is of great significance in the mourning process. It is a way in which we can be encouraged and supported to accept the reality that our loved one has died, at least to this life. We are in a place that reminds me of the words in the hymn 'How Great Thou Art', 'I scarce can take it in.' The theories of phases and stages of grief speak of denial of reality, a reluctance to accept the death. Worden's first task requires us to accept the reality. I should note at this point, in relation to my previous discussion about the euphemisms we use to deny the reality of death, that some of the phrases we use can be an expression of faith rather than a denial of reality. I remember presenting a course on bereavement to a group of Church ministers in Belfast. In the course of our discussions a member of the Salvation Army reminded me that when Salvationists refer to someone who has died as having been promoted to glory, this is not a denial of the reality of death but an expression of faith. In fact, for them it is an affirmation of the reality of death. In 1890 Herbert Booth, son of Salvation Army founder William Booth, penned the hymn, 'Promoted to Glory', which is still used at Salvationist funerals today.

Except for a brief period ministering in North West England, I have lived and worked most of my life in Ireland, and it is within the context of Irish Catholicism that I have learned to mourn. The purpose of a Catholic funeral is threefold:

1. To offer worship, praise and thanksgiving to God for the gift of a life that has now returned to God.
2. To commend the dead to God's merciful love and pray for the forgiveness of their sins.
3. To bring hope and consolation to those who mourn.

The second of these elements is generally absent from funerals in the Reformed Tradition, which believes that there is no point in praying, as Catholics do, that the dead 'may be loosed from their sins' (2 Maccabees 12:46). Indeed, this is in part why the Books of Maccabees are excluded as apocryphal from post-Reformation bibles. A misinterpretation, or misrepresentation, of this particular element in Catholic funerals is why there is often criticism of funerals taking place in Catholic churches for people perceived or judged by others to be separated from God by the way in which they lived their lives. This has been particularly true in relation to so-called paramilitary funerals in Ireland.

The threefold purpose of the Catholic funeral makes me think of the significance of the number *three* in our Christian faith. Belief in *three persons in the one God* has been an integral part of Christian faith since the beginning of the Church, based on Christ's teaching and formalised by the Council of Nicea in 325 AD. In the Nicene Creed, recited at Mass every Sunday, we give voice to our belief in God the Father, Son and Holy Spirit. We begin our prayers and end them in the name of the triune God. We baptise in the name of the Father, Son and Holy Spirit. In the Western Church, on the Sunday following Pentecost Sunday, we celebrate Trinity Sunday. The three-leafed shamrock, so long a symbol associated with Ireland, is reputed to have been used by St Patrick to illustrate the doctrine of the Trinity. Thus, the number three is highly significant. In John's Gospel Jesus told the Jewish leaders of the Temple in Jerusalem, 'Destroy this temple, and *in three days I will raise it up*' (2:19). As John explains, he was referring to the temple of his own body, and when Jesus rose from the dead, his followers remembered that he had said this. Later in John's Gospel (chapter 18) we read how Peter disowned Christ *three times*, but then, in chapter 21, Peter is recorded as making a *threefold* declaration of his love for Christ. Traditionally in Western Christian Churches, including some Anglican, Lutheran, Methodist and Roman Catholic, the Way of the Cross is a popular devotion. The third, seventh and ninth stations refer to Jesus falling *three* times under the weight of his cross.

My mother died on a Saturday and her funeral was held on the following Monday; my father died on a Wednesday and his funeral was on the Friday. This tradition owes its origins to belief in Jesus' resurrection on the *third day*. Of course, it is becoming increasingly more difficult to maintain this tradition with the increasing popularity of cremation and with fewer grave spaces in Church graveyards and more burials taking place in civic cemeteries.

ORDER OF CHRISTIAN FUNERALS

In the Catholic Church, practice around the funeral rites is governed by the *Order of Christian Funerals* prepared by the Congregation for Divine Worship and, with the authority of Pope Paul VI, issued as a Decree in August 1969. It came about as a result of a directive by the Second Vatican Council in the Constitution on the Liturgy 'that the funeral rites be revised in such a way that they more clearly express the paschal character of the Christian's death' (Order of Christian Funerals, pages 81–82). Writing in his introduction to the 1991 edition of the *Order of Christian Funerals*, Cardinal

Cahal Daly says, 'With prayer and ritual, we journey with the body of the deceased, honouring that body and commending the dead to God's merciful love.' He further notes that, 'We also journey with those who mourn, for we recognise the pain of bereavement. This is part of the ministry of consolation ... to care for the dying, to pray for the dead, to comfort those who mourn.' We encounter the number three again in these three elements of what Cardinal Daly described as the ministry of consolation.

The *Order of Christian Funerals* sets out three main stages or stations in the funeral rites of the Catholic Church. These, in effect, would be more accurately described as mourning rites than funeral rites, since they begin immediately following the death.

1   **At the home of the deceased**
    (*or in the funeral home/chapel of rest*)
    There are several short services that may be used in the home.

- **Prayers after death.** This short service generally takes place when the priest/minister first meets with the family after the death. If the priest/minister has been with the family at the time of death it may follow immediately.

- **Gathering in the presence of the body.** Another short service, this usually consists of the reading of a short scripture verse, sprinkling the body with holy water, the recitation of a psalm and the Lord's Prayer, concluding with a prayer and blessing. As it says in the rite, 'The family members, in assembling in the presence of the body, confront in the most immediate way the fact of their loss and the mystery of death' (*Order of Christian Funerals*, page 23).

- **Vigil for the deceased.** This is a more formal service and is particularly appropriate for celebration during the wake. In earlier times the wake was a time when the family, supported by friends, neighbours and their parish community, stayed awake (which is indeed where the word 'wake' has its origins) in vigil for the deceased, praying that they might be loosed from their sins and be welcomed to join with their risen Saviour in the eternal happiness of heaven. Essentially the vigil takes the form of a liturgy of the Word.

The priest, or a lay minister, leads the service with an invitation to prayer and to listen to the word of God. After an opening prayer there is usually a first reading from either the Old Testament or one of the New Testament letters. A psalm is then said or sung followed by a reading from one of the four gospels. This may be followed by a short homily based on the readings. This is an opportunity to reflect on the great mystery of death and the resurrection to eternal life won for us by Christ's own death and resurrection. It is also a time for those present to find consolation, strength and hope in the sacred scriptures.

There then follow prayers of intercession calling on God to comfort those in mourning and to show mercy to the deceased, concluding with the Lord's Prayer, closing prayer and a blessing.

• **Transfer of the body to the church.** When the time has come for the coffin to be closed and the deceased to be taken from home, funeral parlour or mortuary chapel to the church there is a short rite for this transfer or the removal, as it is generally referred to. This is an extremely emotional moment for the family – the last time their loved one leaves the house. There is a tradition among Catholics of having a small holy water font just inside the door of the house. As people leave they dip their hand in the holy water and bless themselves for a safe journey. It is fitting therefore to mark this final journey from the house with a prayer and sprinkling the body with holy water.

The service is simple in nature. Commonly it includes a short scripture verse, the Lord's Prayer, a concluding prayer and an invitation to process to the Church. I would usually sprinkle the body with holy water and make the sign of the cross on the deceased's forehead. I would then invite the family to do the same, if they wish. It is a time when family members can take a quiet moment to say farewell and perhaps kiss their loved one goodbye before the coffin is closed.

This service can be, and often is, led by a lay person or, indeed, the funeral director or a family member. Some people prefer that their priest or other minister leads the prayers and the practice can vary from place to place.

2   At the church (*or crematorium*)

There are essentially two parts to the celebration of the funeral rites at the church.

- **Reception of the body at the church.** According to local custom or the wishes of the family (or the deceased person) this may take place at a time prior to the funeral Mass, usually the evening before, or immediately before the Mass. In my younger days the former was always the case; nowadays, more often than not, the body is brought to the church to arrive for the start of the funeral Mass. Some Catholics favour the idea of spending a night reposing in the church before the Blessed Sacrament prior to the funeral. I have indicated to my family that this would be my wish when my time comes. On a practical level it serves as an opportunity for people to be present who, because of work or for other reasons, cannot attend the actual funeral. In my view it also allows the family to have a night to rest after the wake before facing the funeral the following day.

The format of this celebration follows that of a liturgy of the Word. The coffin is received at the door of the church at which point it is sprinkled with holy water as a reminder of the person's baptism, before being led to a resting place, usually in front of the altar. Where it is customary the coffin may then be draped in a pall as a reminder of the white garment used in baptism. A cross and/or a bible may then be placed on top as symbols of Christian life. These are the only items that should be placed on the coffin. All other items, such as flags or flowers, should be removed at the church entrance and may be replaced after the coffin has been taken from the church at the end of the funeral. The only exceptions allowed in the *Order of Christian Funerals* are 'marks of distinction arising from a person's liturgical function or holy orders and those honours due to civil authorities' (page xi). This can sometimes give rise to debate and disagreement when some individual clergy adopt a more liberal interpretation of this directive than others. There can be a perception of unfairness which can cause upset – the very antithesis of what funeral liturgies should be!

- **The funeral Mass.** The funeral generally takes place at the regular daily celebration of the Eucharist in the parish. Here the parish family gathers with the deceased and those grieving as their brothers and sisters in Christ, to pray with them and support them in their grief. In this way the liturgy for the dead is fit, 'into the total setting of the liturgical life of the parish' as per the guidance in the *Order of Christian Funerals* (page xiii).

When the remains are brought to the church at the time of the of the funeral Mass, the priest receives the coffin at the door of the church, reciting a prayer and sprinkling the coffin with holy water. He and assisting ministers then lead the coffin and mourners into the church and process to the altar to begin the Mass. In these circumstances the reception of the coffin and sprinkling with holy water replace the penitential rite in the Mass and, after welcoming the congregation, the priest says the opening prayer, or collect, of the Mass.

When the deceased has been reposing in the church for a time prior to the funeral, the Mass begins in the normal way with the priest and accompanying ministers processing to the altar. The funeral Mass follows essentially the same structure as the normal Sunday Mass. The priest begins Mass as usual by welcoming the congregation, conducting the penitential rite and saying the opening prayer.

• **The Liturgy of the Word** then follows. Readings from Scripture are chosen to teach remembrance of the dead and to convey the hope of us being reunited in God's kingdom. Above all the scripture readings tell how the pain and suffering of death and sin have been conquered by the death and resurrection of our Saviour, Jesus Christ, and how all the baptised are called to share in that resurrection. Generally, there are two readings and a psalm followed by a reading from one of the gospels. Normally one of the readings chosen is from the Old Testament and the other from the New Testament letters. Following the gospel reading the priest delivers a brief homily based on the readings. This is not a eulogy but an opportunity for catechesis. The priest shares with the mourners the message contained in the scripture that we grieve as people who have hope, hope given to us that, 'as Christ was raised from the dead by the Father's glory, we too might live a new life' (Romans 6:4). Although this is not a eulogy, the priest may 'weave' some biographical stories of the deceased into the homily.

The liturgy of the Word concludes with the prayers of intercession, responding to the proclamation of God's word praying for the deceased and those who mourn. Other intercessions may be included as deemed appropriate.

- **The liturgy of the Eucharist** follows. This is the same as we are accustomed to at any other Mass. Having been nourished by the Word of God in sacred scripture we bring forward the gifts of bread and wine, fruits of the earth and the work of human hands, to be consecrated and fed to us as spiritual nourishment in Holy Communion. It should be noted that the gifts brought forward in the offertory procession should be those to be used in the Eucharistic celebration, namely the bread and wine and the sacred vessels to be used. Other items reflecting interests or hobbies of the deceased are not appropriate for the procession. This occasionally causes some tension, principally I believe because some priests take a laxer approach to the guidelines than others. This can create an impression of some people being treated more favourably than others, especially in the case of a current or former civic leader or celebrity. Some of the items I have seen being brought

41

up include gardening gloves, a football, dancing shoes and, on one occasion, a picture of Elvis Presley!

We move from the Offertory to the Eucharistic Prayer. Versions II and III are particularly appropriate as they contain special texts of intercession for the deceased. After the Lord's Prayer and distribution of Communion the priest says the concluding prayer of the Mass and moves on to the rite of final commendation.

- **Final commendation and farewell.** This is a final farewell by members of the parish family, entrusting their brother/sister to the tender and merciful embrace of God. It begins with the priest or minister inviting the congregation to pray silently for the deceased, during which time the coffin is sprinkled with holy water and incensed. As in other parts of the liturgy the holy water is a symbolic representation of the water of Baptism through which we enter God's family. The use of incense signifies respect for the body as the temple of the Holy Spirit. The fragrant smoke rising heavenwards from the incense is also symbolic of our prayers rising to heaven.

  This is followed by a song of farewell. The one most commonly used is a beautiful testament to our Christian belief in the victory over death and sin won for us by the death and resurrection of Christ.

Saints of God, come to his/her aid!
Hasten to meet him/her angels of the Lord!
R. *Receive his/her soul and*
present him/her to God the Most High.

May Christ, who has called you, take you to himself; may angels lead you to the bosom of Abraham. **R**

Eternal rest grant unto him/her, O Lord,
and let perpetual light shine upon him/her. **R**

At the end of the liturgy a concluding prayer is said
calling on God's mercy, commending the deceased
into God's hands and affirming the belief that those
who have died in Christ will share in Christ's victory
over death.

The priest or minister concludes by saying, 'In peace
let us take our brother/sister to his/her place of rest.'
The mourners, accompanying the coffin, process out
of the church, led by the priest and ministers while an
appropriate hymn is sung.

3   At the cemetery

This is a short rite of committal conducted at the grave,
at the crematorium or indeed during burial at sea. 'In
committing the body to its resting place, the community
expresses the hope that, with all those who have gone
before marked with the sign of faith, the deceased awaits
the glory of the resurrection' (*Order of Christian Funerals*,
97). The rite may be repeated at a later time, for example
when ashes are being interred. The act of committal is a
powerful expression of the separation of the mourners
from the deceased in this life. While the rite may be led
by a minister other than a priest, the stark and final nature
of the burial is such that people generally prefer that their
priest is with them at this time.

The rite consists of a Scripture verse, a prayer over the place
of committal, the committal itself, intercessions, the Lord's
Prayer, a concluding prayer and a final blessing. Depending on
local tradition a decade of the Rosary may be said along with
a hymn or song.

43

SOME CUSTOMS AND PRACTICES AROUND FUNERALS

CREMATION

For many centuries cremation was not favourably viewed in Western society. Indeed, disposal of a body by cremation was made a crime, punishable by death, by Charlemagne in 789. It wasn't until the end of the nineteenth century that cremation ceased to be a crime in Britain, with the first legal cremation taking place in 1885. The Cremation Act of 1902 removed all legal ambiguity and led to the establishment of official crematoria, although the first purpose-built crematorium in England was built in Woking in 1878. It is still in use today. In other parts of Europe there are variations in approach to cremation with the highest proportion of cremations in the EU being in the Czech Republic while, since the fall of communism, cremation has all but disappeared in Poland. In Britain today approximately eighty per cent of funerals are cremations, whereas in Ireland it is the reverse with almost twenty per cent being cremations and eighty per cent burials. Indeed, Ireland's first crematorium wasn't opened until 1961, with the inauguration of Roselawn Crematorium in Belfast. There were no crematoria in the Republic of Ireland until March 1982 when a crematorium was opened in Glasnevin, Dublin.

It is only relatively recently that cremation has become an acceptable practice among Christians generally and Catholics in particular. Belief in the resurrection of the body is a central tenet of the Christian faith and cremation was viewed as denying the doctrine of bodily resurrection. In the years following the First World War, Protestant Churches began gradually to approve cremation. It was only in 1963 that the Catholic Church lifted its ban on cremation, although burial is still the preferred option. The Eastern Orthodox Church still prohibits cremation, as do Orthodox Jews and Muslims.

It is increasingly common for bereaved families to scatter the ashes of a bereaved person in some place with special meaning for them, for example a favourite beauty spot, a river or at sea. Sometimes ashes are scattered over a football pitch or a golf course. Occasionally families choose to divide the ashes among several containers or vessels and distribute them among family members who may decide to keep them in their home or scatter or bury them.

Catholic teaching is that the ashes of a cremated person should not be divided or scattered but should be treated with the same respect and reverence as a body. Ashes should therefore be buried in a grave or placed in a mausoleum or a columbarium. A mausoleum is essentially a tomb above ground. A columbarium is a wall with cavities designed to hold urns containing cremated remains. Some are located within mausoleums, although increasingly many are to be found in a crypt below a church or in a side chapel designated for the purpose. As many of our smaller churches are closed due to falling numbers, I would suggest that some of them could be used as columbaria, especially where they are located within a parish graveyard.

Apart from religious reasons for this way of treating cremated remains, a positive psychological benefit for the bereaved family and friends is that they have a place to visit to remember their loved ones and to pray for them.

MUSIC

The choice of music for the funeral rites can sometimes be contentious. According to the *Order of Christian Funerals*, music is an integral part of the funeral rites. 'It allows the community to express convictions and feelings that words alone may fail to convey' (page 10). The order states that the text of songs chosen should be sacred in nature and express the paschal mystery of Christ's life, death and resurrection.

In communicating this to the grieving family the priest or

minister needs to exercise a degree of tact. A blunt statement that the latest chart hit or most frequently streamed song is simply not allowed may compound the mourners' grief. Suggestions for other more appropriate settings for a particular song may be helpful. I remember a family who wanted a song, 'Maggie', which was a particular favourite of their mother, to be sung during the funeral Mass. It was very obviously not appropriate for the church, but I gently explained why and suggested to the son that they could perhaps sing it later when the family and friends had gathered together after the burial. The suggestion was acceptable, and we avoided any acrimony at a particularly sensitive time. It is perhaps a case of, as an old friend of mine used to say, 'putting a bit of lace around it'!

This directive regarding appropriate music is another of those directives that can be made difficult to implement because of the laxer approach some take, which can create an impression of favouritism.

READINGS

The Word of God is central to the life of any Christian. Indeed, every faith has its sacred writings, whether it be the Christian Bible, the Islamic Koran or the Jewish Torah and Talmud. For all of us, great importance is attached to the reading of the word of God. Every service in the Catholic liturgy contains readings from Sacred Scripture and the liturgy around death and mourning is no exception. No matter at which of the three stations (in the home, church or cemetery) the service occurs, we find scripture readings.

It is important that due respect is given to the proclamation of God's word. In many places it is customary for members of the deceased's family, or friends of the deceased, to read at the services or Mass. While it might be nice to involve as many family members as possible, sometimes an individual's anguish at the death may make it difficult for them to read without breaking down. Sometimes in families there is a 'pecking order', which dictates who should or shouldn't perform a particular role. It might seem obvious, but in selecting readers it is vital that those chosen to read are capable of reading the scriptures with meaning and clarity.

One issue for me is the practice of reading from a booklet or order of service or indeed from a photocopied page. I have seen this happening frequently at both funerals and weddings in Catholic churches. In my thinking, this does not show appropriate honour for God's word. I may come across as pedantic, but my view is that Scripture readings should be proclaimed in church from the lectionary or from a bible.

In choosing the readings for the funeral liturgy it should be remembered that they must be from the Scriptures. Biblical readings may not be replaced by non-biblical readings (*Order of Christian Funerals*, page 8). This is where the priest or other minister can guide the mourners in their selection of suitable and meaningful passages to read. Other readings, such as a favourite poem, may be appropriately used in other settings like the home, funeral parlour or crematorium.

FAMILY PARTICIPATION

It is common practice in Catholic funerals for family members to play an active role, whether this is by reading from the Scriptures, leading prayers of intercession or carrying the gifts of bread and wine to the altar in the Offertory Procession. The same caveat obtains here with regard to how well people are able to participate in this way in the face of their own anguish.

When I worked for Cruse Bereavement Care in Belfast, I became friendly with Reverend Professor Jim Boyd. Jim was a minister in the Presbyterian Church in Ireland. He lectured for many years in Union Theological College in Belfast, where men and women trained for the Presbyterian ministry. Jim and I had many conversations of a theological and pastoral nature. I remember well one of the topics we returned to on several occasions was this practice of family involvement in funerals, and indeed other services such as weddings. Jim was of the view that a funeral service was an occasion for the Church community to minister to this grieving family; if family members were delivering readings or prayers of intercession, they were in effect ministering to themselves. For this reason, Jim never conducted funerals or weddings for his own family circle. I invited Jim to put his thoughts on paper for the *Bereavement Care* journal and his article was published in 1994, sadly posthumously (Vol. 13, No. 2). In the article he suggested that those who conduct funeral services 'should ask themselves whether the family's and others' needs will not be more satisfactorily met by having "expert" leadership through which each part of the service may be fully heard by those present, without the upsurge of unnecessary apprehension and conflicting thoughts.'[6]

I remember a work colleague once telling me that she was reading a Scripture passage at her father's funeral and was so nervous and anxious about 'doing a good job', that she did not take in a single word the priest said before she got up to read. After she sat down again, she was so relieved that she had not 'let herself down', that she missed a lot of what came after.

I hear what Jim and my colleague said and yet I felt it a great honour to conduct my mother's funeral and I have participated in the funerals of other family members and friends over the years. I can see that participation in a loved one's funeral liturgy can be a wonderful healing experience, yet for some it could compound their feelings of confusion, disorganisation and apprehension.

I leave the question out there but would always caution when arranging funerals to be as diligent as possible in ensuring that nobody feels under compunction to participate just because they feel it is expected of them or because they have seen others do it. Grieving people should be supported to say 'No' if they wish, without feeling guilty that they have somehow shirked a duty.

6   *Bereavement Care*, vol. 13, no. 2, 1994, 15.

CHILDREN'S INVOLVEMENT

We need to be aware of the children around us at the time of a death. Children are every bit as much a part of the grieving family as we are and need to be involved to the degree appropriate to their age and development. I always say that if we, as adults, benefit from the rituals of mourning, then surely children too need the benefits to be gained from ritualising their grief. The rituals around mourning outlined previously, through the various services leading up to and culminating in the funeral and final commendation and committal, help us to reinforce the reality, to express our grief and, for those of us with faith, to entrust our loved one to God's loving care and be consoled by each other and by our faith. Children need that too. People often mistakenly shield children from the whole process by having them go and stay with friends or neighbours. This attempt to shield them from the reality of what has happened may only serve to leave them feeling confused and excluded. It is important that we allow children to grieve, to cry and to allow them to see our grief.

It is important that we explain things to children in simple everyday language, avoiding euphemisms. I have heard of children being afraid to go to sleep at night in case they never wake up again. They had been told that their dead Granny had fallen asleep. We need to find words to convey the reality of death without adding to their confusion or bewilderment. If we are feeling too raw ourselves it may even be that we get someone else they know and trust, perhaps a teacher, to explain it to them.

As children develop cognitively, so their understanding of death develops. Very young children may view death as a temporary, reversible thing – perhaps based on their viewing of television cartoons! Psychologists would suggest that by the age of nine or ten, children reach what is known as the nodal point of conceptual development and it is around this time that they begin to realise the reality of death as an irreversible event. This will vary, depending on a number of factors, including how much exposure to death they have had already. Studies in Belfast in the 1980s showed that children in areas of the city where violent death was more common had a more mature understanding of the reality of death than children of a similar age living in more peaceful areas.

When it comes to the funeral there is no valid argument for excluding children. Simply being present may be enough, although very small children will not understand much of what is happening. We should involve them as much as possible, depending on their age and their own wishes. They may be able to carry up some of the gifts in the offertory procession. Older children may be able to read a prayer or read a short poem as a post-Communion reflection. Having said that, children should never be forced to participate, but I believe it is important that they are encouraged to do so.

Different faith traditions have different views and practices in relation to children's participation in funerals or even with regard to being present at funerals. When we took my granddaughter to her great-grandmother's funeral service in a Church of Ireland church she was the only child present. She wanted to be there, and I felt it was important to respect her wishes and to help her begin to process her grief.

Another important factor to consider is the need to sympathise with children. As adults we appreciate expressions of sympathy. A friend of mine took her nine-year-old son to the funeral of his grandfather. On the way home she asked him if he was okay. His reply was, 'Yes. But nobody told me they were sorry my Grandpa was dead.'

The basic rule is, don't ignore or minimise the grief of children or their need to avail of the mourning rituals that we need and appreciate.

∽ CHAPTER 3 ∽

GRIEF IN THE SCRIPTURES

In the beginning was the Word, and the Word was with God,
and the Word was God. (John 1:1)

Having looked at the human experience of grief and the rites of mourning, I turn now to the word of God in the scriptures. In all our liturgies we read from sacred scripture. In our daily celebration of the Mass we come together to be nourished by the Lord in Holy Communion and by his word. In each of the three 'stations' of the liturgies associated with mourning the word of God is central.

Since the loss of innocence experienced by Adam and Eve and the pain of their subsequent banishment from the Garden of Eden, grief has been present in our world. In communicating God's word to us the biblical authors wrote about this pain and God's plan for us. Sometimes they were writing about a specific bereavement through the death of a loved one and, in other instances, about grief experienced in the context of losing or missing God through defeat in battle or through exile.

Of the four gospels, my favourite is the Gospel of John. There is a beautiful poetic nature to the writing, beginning with the prologue (John 1:1–18). The prologue sets out the gospel's theme of God making his presence known in the world and bringing salvation to the world through the incarnation of his Son.

There is a strong link between John's prologue and the very first book of the Bible, Genesis. Both books start with the same three words – 'In the beginning'. The author of Genesis begins by telling us how, through his creative word, God made the world and all that is in it.

God *said,* 'Let there be light.' (1:3)

God *said,* 'Let the earth put forth vegetation.' (1:11)

God *said,* 'Let the earth bring forth living creatures of every kind.' (1:24)

God *said,* 'Let us make humankind in our image.' (1:26)

John's prologue tells us that,

> In the beginning was the Word, and the Word was with God, and the Word was God. (1:1)

In verse 14 of that first chapter we have the most profound statement in all of scripture:

> And the Word became flesh and lived among us.

WHAT HAS THE WORD OF GOD TO SAY ABOUT THE PAIN OF GRIEF?

There are many references in both the Old and New Testaments to these emotional and spiritual reactions to grief.

SORROW

Perhaps the most all-encompassing of our reactions to grief is the overpowering sense of sorrow visited on the bereaved. We encounter this very early on in the scriptures. Jacob speaks of his sorrow at the loss of his sons Joseph and Simeon, and the potential loss of his youngest son, Benjamin.

> … you would bring down my gray hairs with sorrow to Sheol (Genesis 42:38)

Job describes his sorrow thus:

> My eye has grown dim from grief,
> and all my members are like a shadow. (Job 17:7)

The sorrow expressed by Solomon in the Book of Proverbs is a spirit-breaking sadness.

> … by sorrow of heart the spirit is broken. (Proverbs 15:13)

DESPAIR/HOPELESSNESS

In 1981, following the death of his son, Aaron, from a premature ageing disease, Rabbi Harold Kushner published *When Bad Things Happen to Good People*. In his book Kushner addresses the issue of the conflict between a world created by a loving and caring God and the pain and suffering existing within it. In her 1984 novella, *The Only Problem*, Muriel Spark reflects on the problem of suffering in the Book of Job, through the musings of the main protagonist, Harvey Gotham. In the Book of Job, the author laments on the apparent dichotomy between his virtuousness and the misfortune and sickness visited upon him. Job cries out in his despair,

> Why did I not die at birth,
> come forth from the womb and expire? (Job 3:11)

> God gives me up to the ungodly,
> and casts me into the hands of the wicked. (Job 16:11)

Job's despair and hopelessness are similar to what we read in Lamentations:

> my soul is bereft of peace;
>   I have forgotten what happiness is;
> so I say, 'Gone is my glory,
>   and all that I had hoped for from the Lord.'
> (Lamentations 3:17–18)

The Psalms contain many references to despair and hopelessness. In Psalm 13, we read of the sense of despair experienced by the writer, who feels God's absence in the face of defeat by his enemies.

> How long, O Lord? Will you forget me forever?
> How long will you hide your face from me?

> How long must I bear pain in my soul,
> and have sorrow in my heart all day long?
> How long shall my enemy be exalted over me?
> (Psalm 13:1–3)

The opening verse of Psalm 22 is that heartfelt cry of despair echoed by Jesus as he hung on the cross:

> My God, my God, why have you forsaken me? (Mark 15:34)

Cries of despair are also to be found in other parts of Jesus' passion. As he agonised in the Garden of Gethsemane, anticipating what lay before him, he said,

> I am deeply grieved, even to death; (Matthew 26:38)

> My, Father, if it is possible, let this cup pass from me; (Matthew 26:39)

FEAR

There are few fears stronger than the fear of death and dying and the fear that grips us when someone close to us dies. Fear is a common grief reaction and is also a topic addressed frequently by various writers in the Bible. Job describes this strong emotion:

> … the firstborn of death consumes their limbs,
> They are torn from the tent they trusted,
> and are brought to the King of terrors. (Job 18:13–14)

Nehemiah speaks of the grief brought on by his sadness at the destruction of Jerusalem,

> So the king said to me, 'Why is your face sad, since you are not sick? This can only be sadness of the heart.' Then I was very much afraid. (Nehemiah 2:2)

In Psalm 143, the psalmist cries out,

> Therefore my spirit faints within me
> my heart within me is appalled. (Psalm 143:4)

The writer of the Letter to the Hebrews addresses the fear that existed before death was conquered by Christ.

> ... and free those who all their lives were held in slavery by the fear of death. (Hebrews 2:15)

WEEPING/CRYING

Tears are a common release of emotion, whether in sadness or joy. Tears of sadness are part and parcel of our grief as they were for the authors of the books of the Bible. When his wife Sarah died we are told that Abraham

> went in to mourn for Sarah and weep for her. (Genesis 23:2)

When Moses died, just as his people neared the Promised Land, we are told that

> The Israelites wept for Moses in the plains of Moab thirty days; then the period of mourning for Moses was ended. (Deuteronomy 34:8)

In Jewish tradition weeping was often accompanied by the tearing of clothes. This was a sign of the depth of their emotional pain. Three of Job's friends, on hearing of the troubles that had befallen him, set out to offer him sympathy and consolation. When they saw him, they were so overcome with grief that

> [They] wept aloud; they tore their robes ... (Job 2:12)

A particularly descriptive expression of the tears of grief is to be found in Psalm 6:

> I am weary with my moaning;
> > every night I flood my bed with tears;
> > I drench my couch with weeping.
> My eyes waste away because of grief; (Psalm 6:6–7)

For me the most profound, yet simplest, expression of grief manifesting itself through tears is to be found in John's Gospel. Jesus had arrived at the house of his friends Lazarus, Martha and Mary in Bethany. On learning that Lazarus had died, Jesus was sorely distressed and we are told that 'with a sigh that came straight from the heart', he asked where Lazarus had been laid and when they brought him to the place we read the shortest verse in all of scripture:

Jesus wept. (John 11:35)

Seeing his tears, the people around him said, 'See how much he loved him!' (John 11:36).

When I encounter a weeping, grieving person I often think of that shortest of verses, 'Jesus wept', and I reflect on the message contained therein that Jesus has been down the road of grief before us. He knows what grief is; he has experienced it himself.

So far I have focused on the emotional, physical and spiritual pain of grief in Scripture, but the word of God is about nothing if not the positivity flowing from faith – trust, hope, comfort.

FAITH

The people of God in both the Old and New Testaments had a strong faith in God, albeit a faith that was tested at times – not unlike our own! In spite of all the trials and tribulations they had to face they maintained a strong faith in the power, mercy and love of God. They knew that

… and the faithful will abide with him in love,

because grace and mercy are upon his holy ones,
(Wisdom 3:9)

In the New Testament times the author of the Letter to the Hebrews reminds his readers in chapter 12 about the faith of their ancestors and all that their faith achieved. In chapter 13 he exhorts his readers to remain strong in their faith and he reminds them of God's promise not to fail or desert them so that they can have confidence in the words of the Psalmist: 'With the Lord on my side I do not fear' (Psalm 118:6).

TRUST

They trusted that the God in whom they had faith, and who kept faith with them, was always there for them. They believed his word, spoken through the prophet Isaiah:

I will strengthen you, I will help you,
I will uphold you with my victorious right hand. (Isaiah 41:10)

For I, the Lord your God,
hold your right hand;
it is I who say to you, 'Do not fear,
I will help you.' (Isaiah 41:13)

It is a trust arising from faith in God – a trust the Psalmist speaks of, saying,

But I trust in you, O Lord,
I say, 'You are my God.'
My times are in your hand; (Psalm 31:14–15)

That theme of trust carries on into the New Testament. Jesus tells his disciples,

Do not let your hearts be troubled. Believe in God, believe also in me. (John 14:1)

In Mark's Gospel, when the disciples were facing the storm on the Sea of Galilee, they were overcome by fear – much like we sometimes are in the face of grief. Our faith is tested; our trust is shaken. Jesus calmed the storm:

> Then the wind ceased, and there was a dead calm. He said to them, 'Why are you afraid? Have you still no faith?' (Mark 4:39)

St Paul writes to the Christians in Rome,

> ... we even boast in God through our Lord Jesus Christ, through whom we have now received reconciliation. (Romans 5:11)

HOPE

From that trust, of course, springs hope. It is a hope that the author of the Book of Wisdom describes as a hope *full of immortality* (3:4).

In *Mere Christianity* (1952) C. S. Lewis said that Christian hope is not some kind of escapism or wishful thinking. Our Christian faith gives us hope in eternal life. We believe that we will share in Christ's resurrection and live with him forever. This is a genuine, real hope and, as Lewis says, not escapism or wishful thinking. In spite of all the vicissitudes visited upon them, the people of the Old Testament maintained their faith and hope in God's promise of a Saviour, a Messiah.

> Be strong, stand firm, have no fear of them, no terror, for the Lord your God is going with you; he will not fail you or desert you. (Wisdom 31:6)

It was a hope expressed by the writer of Lamentations,

> But this I call to mind,
>   and therefore I have hope:

The steadfast love of the Lord never ceases,
    his mercies never come to an end;
they are new every morning;
great is your faithfulness. (Lamentations 3:21–23)

It is a hope that the psalmist sings of in Psalm 26,

Put your hope in the Lord, be strong, let your heart be bold,
put your hope in the Lord. (Psalm 26:14)

It is the hope given to us by Christ when he said,

In my Father's house there are many dwelling places. If it were not so, would I have told you that I go to prepare a place for you? And if I go and prepare a place for you, I will come again and will take you to myself, so that where I am, there you may be also. (John 14:2–3)

It was also the hope for which Paul was brought before the Sanhedrin after preaching Christ's promise of the resurrection. Paul defended himself and his faith and trust in the hope of the resurrection, given by the teaching, death and resurrection of Christ.

I am on trial concerning the hope of the resurrection of the dead. (Acts 23:6)

It was this message of faith in Christ and belief in Christian hope that Paul preached on his missionary journeys. It transformed the way in which we grieve. Paul wrote to the Church in Thessalonica,

But we do not want you to be uninformed, brothers and sisters, about those who have died, so that you may not grieve them as others do who have no hope. (1 Thessalonians 4:13)

COMFORT

Paul concludes 1 Thessalonians 4 with the following:

> Therefore encourage one another with these words.
> (1 Thessalonians 4:18)

The comfort that comes from God, and his promises to us, is a common theme throughout the Scriptures and is to be found in many of the readings used at funeral services. It is a comfort promised to our ancestors in the Old Testament – a comfort given by God to Joshua when he said,

> I hereby command you: Be strong and courageous; do not
> be frightened or dismayed, for the Lord your God is with
> you wherever you go. (Joshua 1:9)

It is the comfort that God spoke of through the prophet Isaiah when he said,

> do not fear, for I am with you,
>   do not be afraid, for I am your God;
> I will strengthen you, I will help you …
>
> For I, the Lord your God,
>   hold your right hand;
> it is I who say to you, 'Do not fear,
> I will help you.' (Isaiah 41:10–13)

Isaiah 49 tells us that God's care for us is like the care of a woman for her child.

> Can a woman forget her nursing child,
> or show no compassion for the child of her womb?
> Even these may forget,
>   yet I will never forget you. (Isaiah 49:15)

Yes, God assures us,

> I, I am he who comforts you;
> why then are you afraid … (Isaiah 51:12)

The Psalms are a great source of comfort and consolation, and perhaps the best-known psalm and the one most frequently used at funerals is Psalm 23, 'The Lord is my Shepherd'. The entire psalm is a song of joyful trust in the comfort and support that God reaches out to us – he revives our drooping spirit.

> Even though I walk through the darkest valley,
>   I fear no evil;
> for you are with me; (Psalm 23:4)

It ends with that greatest of all comforting promises,

> and I shall dwell in the house of the Lord
> my whole life long. (Psalm 23:6)

Our parish sits at the foot of Slieve Donard, the highest peak in the Mourne Mountains. When we were choosing a strapline to use in parish communications, we opted for the opening verse of Psalm 121. It is a favourite of mine. No matter where we are in the locality all we have to do is raise our eyes heavenward to see the majesty and beauty of God's creation. Indeed, the mountain can be seen from many miles away and when I have been away, as it beckons me homeward, Psalm 121 always come to mind.

> I lift up my eyes to the hills –
>   from where here will my help come?
> My help comes to me from the Lord,
> who made heaven and earth. (Psalm 121:1–2)

The help, comfort and consolation promised is personified in Christ who tells us,

> Peace I leave with you; my peace I give to you. I do not

give to you as the world gives. Do not let your hearts be troubled, and do not let them be afraid. (John 14:27)

And, of course, Jesus tells us in the Beatitudes,

Blessed are those who mourn, for they will be comforted. (Matthew 5:4)

As we grieve for the loss of a loved one we can take comfort in Jesus' promise in John's Gospel:

So you have pain now; but I will see you again, and your hearts will rejoice, and no one will take your joy from you. (John 16:22)

The theme of consolation and comfort is to be found in many of Paul's letters. When delivering courses on bereavement ministry I always begin and end each session with a prayer taken from the opening chapter of Paul's second letter to the Church in Corinth,

Blessed be the God and Father of our Lord Jesus Christ, the Father of mercies and the God of all consolation, who consoles us in all our affliction, so that we may be able to console those who are in any affliction with the consolation with which we ourselves are consoled by God. (2 Corinthians 1:3–4)

For me this reflects what, in his introduction to the *Order of Christian Funerals*, Cardinal Cahal Daly described as the ministry of consolation – caring for the dying, praying for the dead and comforting those who mourn.

In his letter to the Romans, Paul reminds us that, having been baptised in the death of Christ we will share in his resurrection.

But if we have died with Christ, we believe that we will also live with him. We know that Christ, being raised from the dead, will never die again; death no longer has dominion over him. (Romans 6:8–9)

When, in his letter to the Philippians (3:20), Paul tells us that we have a homeland in heaven waiting for us, he echoes that promise by Christ that there are many rooms in his father's house and he has gone to prepare a place for us (John 14:2–3).
And that, in essence, is the source of our comfort.

> I write these things to you who believe in the name of the Son of God, so that you may know you have eternal life. (1 John 5:13)

When I am working with a group training for parish bereavement ministry, I would normally at this stage invite participants to take some time to reflect on which readings from scripture they would choose for their own funeral, or the funeral of a loved one. I invite them to share, in groups of two or three, what they have chosen and what those readings say to them. When we get back together I broaden the discussion to involve us all as a whole group. To get the ball rolling I share my choices.

READINGS AND REFLECTIONS

Book of Lamentations (3:17–25)

> my soul is bereft of peace;
>> I have forgotten what happiness is;
> so I say, 'Gone is my glory,
>> and all that I had hoped for from the Lord.'
> The thought of my affliction and my homelessness
>> is wormwood and gall!
> My soul continually thinks of it
>> and is bowed down within me.
> But this I call to mind,
>> and therefore I have hope:

The steadfast love of the Lord never ceases,
  his mercies never come to an end;
they are new every morning;
  great is your faithfulness.
'The Lord is my portion,' says my soul,
  'therefore I will hope in him.'
The Lord is good to those who wait for him,
  to the soul that seeks him

Reflection

I have chosen this piece from Lamentations even though initially (3:17–20) it seems very morbid. That morbidity reflects so much of how people feel when faced with the pain of grief. We are sad and lack peace in our hearts; we feel weak and hopeless; we are full of anguish and are heartbroken and low in spirit. But, hang on a minute! In verses 21–26 we find the answer to all that. Here is how we recover our hope. We have not been forgotten by God; his favour and his kindness are still there for us. Although in my grief my faith might be shaken, God's faithfulness is constant. If I can just trust in him he will restore my spirit. He will give me peace in my heart; he will give me strength and hope; he will heal my broken heart. That is his promise to us.

In many ways what we have here is the old and the new. The opening chapters of Lamentations have been described as a dirge for the dead. Certainly, the first four verses of our reading reflect that strongly. But what we have next is the antidote to that. Even though it was written some 600 years before the birth of Christ, it anticipates what is to come with the coming of Christ into the world; the Word being made flesh and living among us (John 1:14). It is what the prophet Isaiah foretold when he promised that the child who would be born to us, the son who would be given to us, would bring light to our darkness; would lift the yoke weighing us down. This prince of peace would give us a peace that would never end (Isaiah 9:1–7).

In spite of our grief, this gives us the strength to call out at the end of the reading, 'Thanks be to God!'

Psalm 23

> The Lord is my shepherd, I shall not want.
> He makes me lie down in green pastures;
> he leads me beside still waters;
> he restores my soul.
> He leads me in right paths
> for his name's sake.
> Even though I walk through the darkest valley,
> I fear no evil;
> for you are with me;
> your rod and your staff –
> they comfort me.
> You prepare a table before me
> in the presence of my enemies;
> you anoint my head with oil;
> my cup overflows.
> Surely goodness and mercy shall follow me
> all the days of my life,
> and I shall dwell in the house of the Lord
> my whole life long.

Reflection

This is perhaps the most common of all psalms read or sung at funerals. And no wonder. The comparison of God with a shepherd evokes images of the shepherd caring for his flock; protecting them from danger and harm; of searching out those that were lost. Sheep were important and valuable to the people of Israel and a good shepherd was worth his weight in gold. A good shepherd could identify his own sheep from among many. Shepherds would have slept at night in the fields and hills, caring for and guarding their sheep. A comparison of God with a shepherd is to be found in Ezekiel 34. God was angered by how the people of Israel were like sheep without a shepherd, for their leaders were like poor shepherds, more concerned with looking after themselves than their sheep. God promised to rescue his people from them. 'As a shepherd looks after his scattered flock when he is with them, so will I look after my sheep' (Ezekiel 34:12).

Psalm 23 gives the grieving person some comforting images of the Good Shepherd. One that stands out for me is that picture of the shepherd there with his crook and staff to give me comfort as I travel through the valley of tears and darkness.

And it's not just a source of comfort for me. It is a message about how I can be a comfort to others. It strikes me that we are all called to be God's shepherds. If we accept that call, if we journey with another in their vale of tears, then we can be his 'crook and staff' to give comfort to those who grieve.

2 Timothy 4:6–8

As for me, I am already being poured out as a libation, and the time of my departure has come. I have fought the good fight, I have finished the race, I have kept the faith. From now on there is reserved for me the crown of righteousness, which the Lord, the righteous judge, will give me on that day, and not only to me but also to all who have longed for his appearing.

Reflection

I suppose I chose this short passage from 2 Timothy in the vain hope that it might one day be said of me! I would like to think that when my time comes, it can be said that I have fought the good fight to the end, that I have run the race to the finish and, above all, that I have kept the faith. I believe that we each have a life to lead, that there is a plan of work for each of us to accomplish in this life. There is a myriad different ways in which we are able to respond to Christ's invitation to follow him. We each have a unique good fight to be fought; a unique race to be run. And all of this is under the umbrella of faith.

In the 1992 Olympics in Barcelona, Derek Redmond was

running in the 400 metres semi-final when he had to pull up with a torn hamstring. He was determined to finish and began hopping/ hobbling along. With 100 metres to go he felt a supportive arm around him and heard a familiar voice – his father's. His father helped him to the finish line, to a standing ovation from the spectators. He came in last and was in fact disqualified for having 'outside assistance'. But he ran the race to the finish. When the 'righteous judge' looks at our life, he won't be judging whether we came first or last – simply that we ran the race to the end. Even with, or indeed especially with, the help of our Father.

When Jesus was carrying his heavy cross to Calvary he fell under the weight of it because of his weakness, but each time he fell, he got up again and carried on. Shortly after his inauguration as President of South Africa, Nelson Mandela was interviewed by Fr Brian D'Arcy, who just happened to meet him coming out of a radio studio in South Africa. In the course of the interview, Fr Brian asked him to respond to the popular perception of him as a saint. Mandela pondered for a moment before replying, 'I am not sure what a saint is. I am not a Christian. But somebody once told me that a saint is a sinner who tries harder. If that is the case, then I am indeed a saint.'[7] *So maybe sainthood beckons me! I don't think any of us can want for more than for it to be said of us at our death, 'He has fought the good fight to the end; He has run the race to the finish. He has kept the faith.'*

John's 14:1–6

'Do not let your hearts be troubled. Believe in God, believe also in me. In my Father's house there are many dwelling places. If it were not so, would I have told you that I go to prepare a place for you? And if I go and prepare a place for you, I will come again and will take you to myself, so that where I am, there you may be also. And you know the way to the place where I am going.' Thomas said to him, 'Lord,

7 *Bereavement Care*, vol. 13, no. 2, 1994, 15.

we do not know where you are going. How can we know the way?' Jesus said to him, 'I am the way, and the truth, and the life. No one comes to the Father except through me.

Reflection

In my first reading, the author of Lamentations told us that the Lord is good to those who trust him. Psalm 23 ends with those beautiful words, 'I shall dwell in the house of the Lord my whole life long.' Then, in my second reading, Paul, in his second letter to Timothy, assures us that, having run the race and kept the faith, the crown of righteousness awaits us. And now we have this beautiful analogy in John's Gospel of the mansion that is heaven, with many rooms and one prepared for me. Yes, Jesus has gone on ahead to make it ready for my arrival. That's where the crown of righteousness, spoken of by Paul, awaits.

Thomas, of course, has a question. This is the same apostle who later on (John 20:24–29) refuses to believe the others when they tell him Jesus is risen. This time he wants to know the way to this lovely mansion. And Jesus' response is simple: 'I am the way.' Yes, the way to get there is through Jesus. 'No one can come to the Father except through me.' It's all about trusting in him, about fighting the good fight to the end and running the race to the finish. In essence it's about following the words spoken by Mary to the stewards at the wedding feast in Cana, way back at the start of John's Gospel when Jesus was beginning his ministry. 'Do whatever he tells you' (John 2:5). Yes, we need to listen to all that Jesus has taught us and live accordingly – in short, keep the faith.

It is my hope that when my time comes to pass from this world to the next, that my trust is rewarded; that my hope is fulfilled; that it can be said that I ran the race to the finish; that I kept the faith and that I have followed the Way of Jesus and am now headed for that room that Jesus has prepared for me in his Father's mansion.

∽ CHAPTER 4 ∽

SUGGESTED READINGS, REFLECTIONS AND PRAYERS

OLD TESTAMENT (SOME FIRST READINGS)

A reading from the Book of Exodus (23:20–23)

I am going to send an angel in front of you, to guard you on the way and to bring you to the place that I have prepared. Be attentive to him and listen to his voice; do not rebel against him, for he will not pardon your transgression; for my name is in him.

But if you listen attentively to his voice and do all that I say, then I will be an enemy to your enemies and a foe to your foes.

The Word of the Lord

Reflection

This lovely little passage from Exodus recounts God's promise to his people as he led them from the suffering of slavery in Egypt to the freedom of the Promised Land. Today he is leading us from slavery in a world of sin, pain and suffering to the peace and love of his kingdom in heaven. For me it resonates with John's Gospel passage (14:2–3) in which Jesus talks to his disciples about going before them to prepare a place for them, so that where he is, they may be too. And that is what he has done for N.

It is a truly wonderful promise, and while it may not feel like it today for us in the depths of grief as we mourn the death of N, it is worth reflecting on the heavenly promise laid out for us all. God promised his people during the Exodus that he would send his angel, 'to guard you on the way and to bring you to the place I have prepared'. In our time he has sent his Son, our Saviour, to guard us and bring us to the place he has prepared for us – not the promised land of Canaan, flowing with milk and honey, but a much more bountiful place; our new home in heaven. It is what St Paul described to the Philippians as our homeland in heaven, where 'he will transform the body of our humiliation that it may be conformed to the body of his glory' (Philippians 3:21).

And so, as we gather to mourn the death of N, we pray that he/she will enjoy eternal happiness in heaven, led there by the angel of God guarding him/her as he/she goes.

A reading from the Book of Wisdom (3:1–9)

But the souls of the righteous are in the hand of God,
and no torment will ever touch them.
In the eyes of the foolish they seemed to have died,
and their departure was thought to be a disaster,
and their going from us to be their destruction;
but they are at peace.
For though in the sight of others they were punished,
their hope is full of immortality.
Having been disciplined a little, they will receive great good,
because God tested them and found them worthy of himself;
like gold in the furnace he tried them,
and like a sacrificial burnt offering he accepted them.
In the time of their visitation they will shine forth,
and will run like sparks through the stubble.
They will govern nations and rule over peoples,

and the Lord will reign over them forever.
Those who trust in him will understand truth,
and the faithful will abide with him in love,
because grace and mercy are upon his holy ones,
and he watches over his elect.

The Word of the Lord

Reflection

*In Judaism there was a belief that sickness and death were some
kind of punishment for sin. Elsewhere in the Old Testament it
was a belief that caused a lot of angst to poor Job. Many found
it a difficult concept to accept. It was still around in Jesus' time;
in John's Gospel (9:2) people asked Jesus about a man born
blind, 'Who sinned, this man or his parents?' Jesus was quick to
contradict their view.*

*The author of the Book of Wisdom likewise contradicted that
view. He tells us that 'though they were punished, their hope is full
of immortality' (3:4). No matter how much we suffer in this life, no
matter that the death of our loved one looks like a disaster, their
leaving us like annihilation, that cannot be compared to the peace
that comes after death. Our sufferings are minor compared to the
blessings that await us.*

*God's vision of death is not humankind's. Because of God's
promise to us we possess an immortality that transcends the
human experience of death. 'In the eyes of the foolish they
seemed to have died.' Death is not the end. In the preface of the
funeral Mass the priest prays, 'Indeed for your faithful, Lord,
life is changed, not ended.' In his first letter to the Corinthians,
St Paul talks about Christ as the power and the wisdom of God
(1:25). God's wisdom, he tells us, is really the opposite of human
wisdom. In the suffering and death of Christ, God chose what is
foolish in the sight of men to demonstrate his power and strength;
the death and resurrection of his Son; 'What no eye has seen,*

71

nor ear heard, nor the human heart conceived, what God has
prepared for those who love him' (1 Corinthians 2:9).

The last verse of our reading from Wisdom sums up what this all
means for us. 'Those who trust in him will understand truth, and
the faithful will abide with him in love, because grace and mercy
are upon his holy ones, and he watches over his elect' (3:9).

A reading from the Book of Wisdom (4:7–15)
*(This reading is particularly appropriate for the funeral of a child
or a younger adult.)*

But the righteous, though they die early, will be at rest.
For old age is not honoured for length of time,
or measured by number of years;
but understanding is grey hair for anyone,
and a blameless life is ripe old age.
There were some who pleased God and were loved by him,
and while living among sinners were taken up.
They were caught up so that evil might not change their
    understanding
or guile deceive their souls.
For the fascination of wickedness obscures what is good,
and roving desire perverts the innocent mind.
Being perfected in a short time, they fulfilled long years;
for their souls were pleasing to the Lord,
therefore he took them quickly from the midst of wickedness.
Yet the peoples saw and did not understand,
or take such a thing to heart,
that God's grace and mercy are with his elect,
and that he watches over his holy ones.

The Word of the Lord

Reflection

We find it difficult to accept any loss, but the death of a child or a young person is especially hard to cope with. There is something inherently wrong in a parent having to bury their child. It is out of the natural order of things. It seems so unfair.

When a child dies people try to comfort the grieving parents with pious platitudes, meant to soothe the broken heart, but which in reality do no such thing. How often, for example, have we heard that God only chooses the best flowers for his garden, or that we now have a little angel in heaven. I don't want an angel in heaven, I want him/her with me. 'He's/She's in a better place.' Oh yeah! I'm not feeling that just now. What better place is there for a child than with his/her loving parents?

In our society a widow is a woman whose husband has died; a widower is a man whose wife has died; an orphan is a child whose parent has died. And yet we do not have a word for a parent whose child has died. Is this because it is such a terrible loss to comprehend? Psychologist and psychoanalyst Erich Fromm put it well when he said, 'To die is poignantly bitter, but the idea of having to die without having lived is unbearable.'[8]

In this reading from the Book of Wisdom, we are assured that length of days is not what constitutes old age in the eyes of God. 'A blameless life is ripe old age.' 'Being perfected in a short time, they fulfilled long years'. At the moment we may find it hard to take on board the thoughts expressed so eloquently by the author of the Book of Wisdom. As he says, we are looking on, uncomprehending.

What I sometimes find helpful is reflecting on the experience of Mary, the mother of Jesus. When Jesus was a twelve-year-old boy, Joseph and Mary took him with them on a pilgrimage up to Jerusalem (Luke 2:41–52). During their time there, they became separated from him. One can only imagine their anguish at having lost their son and then their joy at finding him again. Just over twenty years later, as Jesus was dying on the cross, John's Gospel

---

8   Erich Fromm, *Man for Himself*, (New York: Rinehart, 1947).

paints a picture for us of Mary standing at the foot of the cross gazing up at her beloved son (John 19:25). Imagine her grief and heartache at the terrible suffering of her son; of the horrific death he was enduring. With barely moments of his earthly life left, Jesus then gave us his mother to be our mother (19:27). I like to think of Mary as this sorrowing mother who, having walked that difficult path of grief for her son, is there now for us, to support us in our grief.

A reading from the Book of Ecclesiastes (3:1–11)

For everything there is a season, and a time for every matter under heaven:

> a time to be born, and a time to die;
> a time to plant, and a time to pluck up what is planted;
> a time to kill, and a time to heal;
> a time to break down, and a time to build up;
> a time to weep, and a time to laugh;
> a time to mourn, and a time to dance;
> a time to throw away stones, and a time to gather stones together;
> a time to embrace, and a time to refrain from embracing;
> a time to seek, and a time to lose;
> a time to keep, and a time to throw away;
> a time to tear, and a time to sew;
> a time to keep silence, and a time to speak;
> a time to love, and a time to hate;
> a time for war, and a time for peace.

What gain have the workers from their toil? I have seen the business that God has given to everyone to be busy with. He has made everything suitable for its time; moreover he has put a sense of past and future into their minds, yet they cannot find out what God has done from the beginning to the end.

The Word of the Lord

Reflection

I'm old enough to remember the Byrds' interpretation of this passage in their 1965 hit album, Turn, Turn, Turn. *I suppose there are people out there who imagine that the lyrics have their origins with Joni Mitchell or the Byrds! It is a piece of Scripture that speaks to all of us, believers and unbelievers alike.*

In my garden there are wild roses growing up through the hedge at the front of the house. When I'm cutting the hedge I always leave the bit with the roses untouched. I know to leave the pruning back of the roses to either around St Patrick's Day or September/ October. That way I can expect a fine display of blooms in the following summer. Gardeners and farmers are well aware of seasonal changes and the need for certain jobs to be done in particular seasons. There is a time for planting and a time for uprooting what has been planted.

Our lives are governed by time – minutes, hours, days, weeks, months, seasons, years. And just as our years are divided up into seasons and months, our entire lives are divided into other 'seasons' – infancy, childhood, teenage years, adulthood, middle age, old age. My ten-year-old granddaughter told me recently that she is a 'pre-teen'!

This passage in Ecclesiastes, also called the Wisdom of Solomon, speaks to us of the many complex 'seasons' of our lives. There are times when we laugh and smile; when we dance; when we love; when we enjoy peace. Conversely there are times when we cry; when we mourn; when we find ourselves in the midst of war or suffering; when we feel unloved. We cannot enjoy the beauty of a glorious sunrise without going through the darkness of night. We can't appreciate the colours of a beautiful rainbow without the rain.

As Solomon says, there is a time for giving birth and a time for dying. There is a time for mourning and a time for dancing. As we gather in mourning at the death of N we reflect on our faith that as surely as day follows night, eternal life follows earthly death. We

75

cannot enter into eternal life with God without death here. St Paul reminds us in his letter to the Romans that 'having died with Christ we shall return to life with him' (Romans 6:8).

A Reading from the Prophet Isaiah (46:14–16)

But Zion said, 'The Lord has forsaken me,
    my Lord has forgotten me.'
Can a woman forget her nursing child,
    or show no compassion for the child of her womb?
Even these may forget,
    yet I will not forget you.
See, I have inscribed you on the palms of my hands;
    your walls are continually before me.

The Word of the Lord

Reflection

We are well used to hearing God described as a loving father. When Jesus' disciples asked him to teach them to pray he taught them to pray to God as their Father, he taught them to pray, 'Our Father who art in Heaven ... '. The scriptures are peppered with examples of God as father. In Psalm 103 we read, 'As a father has compassion for his children, so the Lord has compassion for those who fear him', and in Matthew's Gospel Jesus says, 'Is there anyone among you who, if your child asks for bread, will give a stone?'

In this reading from the prophet Isaiah we find God's love for us being compared to that of a loving mother. A mother's love is faithful; it is protective; it is sacrificial. The maternal instinct of a mother is to protect her children, to nurture them and to sacrifice her own needs to better meet the needs of her children.

It is common for us, in the depths of grief, to feel abandoned or forgotten by God, but Isaiah is saying, 'Here, hold on a minute, can you imagine a mother abandoning the child at her breast? Well, even if that happens, God's love for you is so intense that he could never abandon or forget you.' In fact, Isaiah goes on to describe that bond as like having you branded or carved on the palm of his hand. There is absolutely no way he could deny you.

So, when we are groaning under the weight of our grief we can take comfort in this promise. It reminds me of the old Irish blessing, 'May the road rise to meet you.' It ends with the words, 'And until we meet again may God hold you in the palm of his hand.' I don't know if that blessing is inspired by the last verse of our reading, but I like to think it might be.

A Reading from the Second Book of Maccabees (12:43–45)

He also took up a collection, man by man, to the amount of two thousand drachmas of silver, and sent it to Jerusalem to provide for a sin offering. In doing this he acted very well and honorably, taking account of the resurrection. For if he were not expecting that those who had fallen would rise again, it would have been superfluous and foolish to pray for the dead. But if he was looking to the splendid reward that is laid up for those who fall asleep in godliness, it was a holy and pious thought. Therefore he made atonement for the dead, so that they might be delivered from their sin.

The Word of the Lord

Reflection
A central aspect of our Catholic funeral liturgies is praying for the happy repose of the soul of the person who has died, and that is at the heart of our celebration of this funeral mass for N. As time goes by we will remember N with Mass and prayers at times like the Month's Mind, anniversaries and occasions such as cemetery Sunday. These prayers and services are particularly Catholic in

nature and this passage from the Book of Maccabees is one of the places where scripture gives us a basis for this. As the writer says, we pray for our deceased brother/sister, taking full account of the resurrection. We read about how a sacrifice was being offered for sin. So yes, we celebrate N's life, we pray for consolation in our grief, but we also give thanks for the redemption won for us by Christ and pray that N will be forgiven any wrong he/she may have committed in this life.

Of course, in our Mass we recall, we make present again, the ultimate sacrifice for sin – the death and resurrection of Christ. It is in taking full account of the resurrection that St Paul was able to say in his first letter to the Thessalonians that we grieve as a people who have hope.

RESPONSORIAL PSALMS

Psalm 25:6–7, 17–18, 20–21; R. v1

Response: To you, O Lord, I lift up my soul.

Be mindful of your mercy, O Lord, and of your steadfast love,
for they have been from of old.
According to your steadfast love remember me,
for your goodness' sake, O Lord! **R**

Relieve the troubles of my heart,
and bring me out of my distress.
Consider my affliction and my trouble,
and forgive all my sins. **R**

O guard my life, and deliver me;
do not let me be put to shame, for I take refuge in you.
May integrity and uprightness preserve me,
for I wait for you. **R**

Reflection

For me the most important part of what the late Cardinal Cahal Daly describes as the ministry of consolation, is the funeral Mass and the other prayers after a death that form what I call the liturgy of mourning. As well as offering prayers for our own consolation and for the strength to cope with our grief, praying for the happy repose of the soul of the deceased is integral to these prayers. The first verse of this extract from Psalm 25 could be spoken by any one of us, particularly as we face the end of our time on this earth. It is in essence a prayer for God's grace and forgiveness for our sins. It is a heartfelt plea for God's mercy. Today we make that prayer on behalf of N as we say (sing), 'Be mindful of your mercy, O Lord, and of your steadfast love, for they have been from of old.' As we move on through the psalm we can turn our thoughts to our own needs. The psalmist could almost be echoing how we feel as he pleads, 'Relieve the troubles of my heart and bring me out of my distress.' It can sometimes be difficult to find God in the midst of our pain. We feel his absence and can call out as Jesus himself did on the cross, 'My God, my God, why have you forsaken me?'

The plea to God not to forget us and to deliver us from pain is a frequent plea found in the Psalms and in many of the other books of the Old Testament. We are, I'm sure, all aware of the pleadings of Job as he wrestled with his afflictions. As we wrestle with our grief today we pray with the psalmist, 'Do not let me be put to shame, for I take refuge in you.'

Psalm 27:1, 4, 7, 9, 13, 14; R v.1

Response: The Lord is my light and my salvation.

The Lord is my light and my salvation;
whom shall I fear?
The Lord is the stronghold of my life;
of whom shall I be afraid? **R**

One thing I asked of the Lord,
that will I seek after:
to live in the house of the Lord
all the days of my life,
to behold the beauty of the Lord,
and to inquire in his temple. **R**

Hear, O Lord, when I cry aloud,
be gracious to me and answer me!
Your face, Lord, do I seek.
Do not hide your face from me. **R**

I believe that I shall see the goodness of the Lord
in the land of the living.
Wait for the Lord;
be strong, and let your heart take courage;
wait for the Lord! **R**

Reflection

In this reading, selected from Psalm 27, it strikes me that some verses could be spoken by the person who has died, some by those who grieve and some by all of us. It begins with an affirmation of truths that all Christians believe, 'The Lord is my light and my salvation', and 'the Lord is the stronghold of my life.' At a time of grief it is easy to feel the absence of God in our breaking hearts, within our aching breast. But when we can embrace this truth that the Lord is our light and our help and our stronghold, then the other elements of those verses hold true as well. What is there to fear? From what need we shrink?

Yes, it is hard to truly feel this at times. But that is one of the reasons that we, as a parish family and your friends, gather round you to support you with our presence and our prayers. We will be the Lord's light and help and stronghold for you.

We also join with you and with N in praying that he/she will savour the sweetness of the Lord and live with him in his house eternally. We implore God to hear our voice, to listen when we call and to show us his mercy.

In funeral Masses and the various prayers we make for our dead, we pray to God to show mercy to the deceased and to give his consolation to us who grieve. All of that is to be found in this reading from Psalm 26.

Psalm 51: 1–7; R. v.1

Response: Have mercy on me, God, in your kindness.

Have mercy on me, O God,
blot out my transgressions.
Wash me thoroughly from my iniquity,
and cleanse me from my sin. **R**

For I know my transgressions,
and my sin is ever before me.
Against you, you alone, have I sinned,
and done what is evil in your sight. **R**

So that you are justified in your sentence
and blameless when you pass judgment.
Indeed, I was born guilty,
a sinner when my mother conceived me. **R**

You desire truth in the inward being;
therefore teach me wisdom in my secret heart.
Purge me with hyssop, and I shall be clean;
wash me, and I shall be whiter than snow. **R**

Reflection

This psalm, the Miserere, is one of the best known of the penitential psalms. It has been set to music by various composers over the centuries, most notably Gregorio Allegri and Mozart. It is a regular part of Jewish and Christian liturgies and is traditionally sung in the Sistine Chapel during Holy Week.

It is regarded as a model for repentance. Right from the very beginning the author, widely believed to be David, acknowledges his sinfulness – my offences; my guilt; my sin. At first look this might seem very negative, but the flip side of that acknowledgement of sin is an acknowledgement of God's mercy and forgiveness. 'Purge me with hyssop, and I shall be clean; wash me, and I shall be whiter than snow.'

Water and washing play an important part in our lives. During the Covid-19 pandemic we were admonished to wash our hands regularly as part of our battle against infection. Water and washing also play an important part in our liturgies. On Holy Thursday we re-enact the ritual washing of the feet of his disciples by Jesus. We begin our Mass with the penitential rite, acknowledging our sins and asking God for his forgiveness. 'Wash me thoroughly from my iniquity, and cleanse me from my sin.' Sometimes the penitential rite includes the ritual sprinkling with holy water. At the Offertory the priest washes his hands, saying, 'Wash me, O Lord, from my iniquity and cleanse me from my sins', echoing the words of our psalm. During the prayers of the final commendation later we will again sprinkle N's body with holy water.

So, as we offer this Mass today, yes we celebrate N's life with us, yes we pray for consolation in our grief, but we also pray for forgiveness, for ourselves and for N. After all, isn't it a holy and a wholesome thought to pray for the dead, that they might be loosed from their sins? (cf. 2 Maccabees12:43–45).

Psalm 121; R v.2

Response: Our help comes from the Lord, who made heaven and earth.

> I lift up my eyes to the hills –
> from where will my help come?
> My help comes from the Lord,
> who made heaven and earth. **R**
>
> He will not let your foot be moved;
> he who keeps you will not slumber.
> He who keeps Israel
> will neither slumber nor sleep. **R**
>
> The Lord is your keeper;
> the Lord is your shade at your right hand.
> The sun shall not strike you by day,
> nor the moon by night. **R**
>
> The Lord will keep you from all evil;
> he will keep your life.
> The Lord will keep
> your going out and your coming in
> from this time on and forevermore. **R**

Reflection

Of all the psalms this is one of my favourites. There is hardly a day in life that I don't look up to the mountains where I live. There is a tremendous beauty to be found there; a beauty that changes with the seasons and yet is constant at the same time. I find it impossible to look up to the mountains and not contemplate the wonder of God. If you stand on the ninth tee of Royal County Down Golf Club in Newcastle your eyes are drawn inexorably to

Slieve Donard rising up in front of you. A man I once knew, an elder in our local Presbyterian church, used to say that every time he stood there he prayed the first verse of this psalm – although I'm not sure it improved his golf!

This psalm is suggested as one of those appropriate to be sung as the body is carried from the church at the end of the funeral Mass. It speaks of comfort and reassurance at a time when we are experiencing fear, anxiety and helplessness; a time when we are grieving. For me it carries a promise of protection and care. Yes, in the midst of all my anxiety and grief the Lord will be by my side, He will be my guard; he will shade me from troubles; he will be there, night and day; he will not fall asleep on the job! At those times when I wonder where, oh where, my help is to come from, I lift up my eyes to the mountain and realise that my help comes from the Lord, the Lord who made heaven and earth.

Psalm 130; R v.1

Response: Out of the depths I cry to you, O Lord.

> Out of the depths I cry to you, O Lord.
> Lord, hear my voice!
> Let your ears be attentive
> to the voice of my supplications! **R**

> If you, O Lord, should mark iniquities,
> Lord, who could stand?
> But there is forgiveness with you,
> so that you may be revered. **R**

> I wait for the Lord, my soul waits,
> and in his word I hope;
> my soul waits for the Lord
> more than those who watch for the morning. **R**

O Israel, hope in the Lord!
For with the Lord there is steadfast love,
and with him is great power to redeem.
It is he who will redeem Israel
from all its iniquities. **R**

Reflection

I remember this psalm from my youth. It was a common Lenten psalm and known by its opening words in Latin, 'De Profundis'. It is prayed every Wednesday in Night Prayer from the Divine Office, or Prayer of the Church. 'De Profundis' is also a title given by some writers to works of poetry or prose. Christina Rossetti wrote a poem called 'De Profundis', and Oscar Wilde's letter, written to Lord Alfred Douglas whilst Wilde was in Reading Gaol, was published with the title De Profundis.

It's not often that Oscar Wilde is cited in a church homily, but this piece from De Profundis *strikes a chord with me.*

> *There is still something to me almost incredible in the idea of a young Galilean peasant imagining that he could bear on his own shoulders the burden of the entire world; all that had already been done and suffered, and all that was yet to be done and suffered ... and not merely imagining this, but actually achieving it.*[9]

Here I see the essence of our belief in Jesus Christ as Saviour and Redeemer. He has taken on his shoulders all the sin and suffering of the world, and by conquering death through his crucifixion and resurrection he has saved us. And that is why we can confidently cry out, from the depths, with the psalmist, 'Lord hear my voice!' And we can make that cry in confidence because we know that we can count on his word and we know that 'with the Lord there is mercy and fullness of redemption'.

9   Oscar Wilde, *De Profundis.*

This psalm is so appropriate for use at a funeral. It encapsulates our plea for help in the depths of our grief and our confident prayer for our loved one as we pray for the happy repose of his/her soul. Because with the Lord is found forgiveness, and for this we revere him.

Psalm 143; R v.1

Response: Lord, listen to my prayer.

Hear my prayer, O Lord;
give ear to my supplications in your faithfulness;
answer me in your righteousness.
Do not enter into judgment with your servant,
for no one living is righteous before you. **R**

I remember the days of old,
I think about all your deeds,
I meditate on the works of your hands.
I stretch out my hands to you;
my soul thirsts for you like a parched land. **R**

Answer me quickly, O Lord;
my spirit fails.
Let me hear of your steadfast love in the morning,
for in you I put my trust. **R**

Teach me to do your will,
for you are my God.
Let your good spirit lead me
on a level path. **R**

Reflection

In our grief we often feel empty; we feel an absence of God; of his helping hand; of his guiding spirit. We fear for the future. This psalm is a heartfelt plea to God to give us his saving help – to listen to our prayer. The psalmist echoes what many of us feel when he says, 'My soul thirsts for you like a parched land.' Yes, we have people around us supporting us but it is somehow not enough.

It reminds me of the line in the prayer of St Gertrude, 'There are times when humans help, but there are times when we need a higher power to assist us bear what must be borne.' We gather today to celebrate and give thanks for the life of N and to pray for the happy repose of his/her soul. We are also imploring God to give us the strength to face today and to face the days to come and whatever fears we have for those days. We pray with the psalmist, 'Let me hear of your steadfast love, for in you I put my trust', and again, 'Let your good spirit lead me on a level path.' And we make these prayers with faith that they will be answered and God will be with us because as it says in the psalm we put our trust in God.

So, in our grief we pray that God will make haste and help us or, as St Gertrude's prayer ends, 'hold on to my trembling hand and be near me today'.

New Testament
(Some Second Readings)

A Reading from the Book of Revelation (21:1–7)

Then I saw a new heaven and a new earth; for the first heaven and the first earth had passed away, and the sea was no more. And I saw the holy city, the new Jerusalem, coming down out of heaven from God, prepared as a bride adorned for her husband. And I heard a loud voice from the throne saying,

'See, the home of God is among mortals.

He will dwell with them;
they will be his peoples,
and God himself will be with them;
he will wipe every tear from their eyes.
Death will be no more;
mourning and crying and pain will be no more,
for the first things have passed away.'
And the one who was seated on the throne said, 'See, I am
making all things new.' Also he said, 'Write this, for these
words are trustworthy and true.' Then he said to me, 'It is
done! I am the Alpha and the Omega, the beginning and
the end. To the thirsty I will give water as a gift from the
spring of the water of life. Those who conquer will inherit
these things, and I will be their God and they will be my
children.

The Word of the Lord

Reflection

The Book of Revelation contains the writer's vision of heaven. I
think we all have our own picture of what heaven may be like. I
remember, as a child, thinking of heaven as a place where true
happiness existed in the form of a huge ice cream shop where you
could have as much as you wanted, and it was all free! Sometimes
it was like a huge room full of toys for endless play!

In Judaism, Jerusalem was the holy city. It was there that God
resided in the Holy of Holies in the Temple, accessible only to
the priests of the Temple. The vision of heaven in Revelation is
of a new Jerusalem where we live with God; where he is our God
and we are his people; where we all have access to him. This is
our inheritance, won for us by God's Son, the Lamb of God. The
picture presented is of a place devoid of any suffering – where
all tears will have been wiped away, where there will be no more
death, nor mourning, nor sadness. And it is a place not just devoid

of suffering, but a place full of love and of life; a place where we will have a free supply of water from the well of life.

I recall a story I heard once concerning a man who had his own business. He used bring his faithful dog to work with him every day. The dog would lie in his basket in front of his master's desk, being fed the occasional treat and being taken out for a walk at lunchtime. The man's business grew and eventually he decided to move to new, larger premises. While the move was happening, the dog stayed at home for a few days until the man's new office was sorted. When all was ready the man's wife brought the dog in and up to the door of the man's new office. As soon as she opened the door, the dog, his tail wagging with joy, bounded in and over to the man. Now the dog had no idea what this new place was like. He had never been there before. The only thing he knew for sure was that his master was waiting for him on the other side of the door.

I can't tell you what heaven is like. I somehow suspect it's not a huge ice cream shop or a big playroom! The author of Revelation couldn't paint a clear picture of what heaven is like either. He did his best to describe the infinite in the limited language of the finite. The only thing we can say for sure is that our Master waits for us on the other side.

A Reading from the Letter of St Paul to the Romans (8:14–23)

For all who are led by the Spirit of God are children of God. For you did not receive a spirit of slavery to fall back into fear, but you have received a spirit of adoption. When we cry, 'Abba! Father!' it is that very Spirit bearing witness with our spirit that we are children of God, and if children, then heirs, heirs of God and joint heirs with Christ – if, in fact, we suffer with him so that we may also be glorified with him.

I consider that the sufferings of this present time are not worth comparing with the glory about to be revealed to us. For the creation waits with eager longing for the revealing of the children of God; for the creation was subjected to futility, not of its own will but by the will of the one who subjected it, in hope that the creation itself will be set free from its bondage to decay and will obtain the freedom of the glory of the children of God. We know that the whole creation has been groaning in labor pains until now; and not only the creation, but we ourselves, who have the first fruits of the Spirit, groan inwardly while we wait for adoption, the redemption of our bodies.

The Word of the Lord

Reflection

When my father died some years ago, I was the executor of his will. It was my job to distribute whatever he had left according to his wishes as expressed in his will. It was a relatively simple task as he just wanted any money in his accounts divided equally among his children. We were his heirs and coheirs with each other. We inherited jointly from him. It wasn't that we had earned that inheritance or that any act of ours had entitled us to inherit. It was simply that as his children we were his heirs and as such we received what he gave of his own will. St Paul tells us in this reading that, as children of God, we are his heirs and coheirs with his Son, Jesus Christ.

So, what do we inherit? Well, essentially it is freedom; freedom from slavery to sin; freedom from the pain and suffering of this life and freedom to enjoy a whole new enriched life with Christ in heaven. Our lives here on earth are a mixture of moments of happiness and of sorrow, of joy and of distress. We will remember the year 2020 as a year with more than its share of sorrow and distress, even if at times we have been inspired by the love and care shown by so many people in our society.

Eternal life, everlasting life, is not simply a continuation of earthly life for ever and ever. If it were, we probably wouldn't long for it or, as St Paul says here, we wouldn't be longing, we wouldn't be groaning as if in one great act of giving birth. This image of childbirth that St Paul uses strikes me as something powerful. I think of the pain of childbirth contrasted with the love and joy that a newborn child brings to a family, a small foretaste of the infinite love and joy that we will inherit as children of God.

A Reading from the First Letter of St Paul to the Corinthians (13:1–8)

If I speak in the tongues of mortals and of angels, but do not have love, I am a noisy gong or a clanging cymbal. And if I have prophetic powers, and understand all mysteries and all knowledge, and if I have all faith, so as to remove mountains, but do not have love, I am nothing. If I give away all my possessions, and if I hand over my body so that I may boast, but do not have love, I gain nothing.

Love is patient; love is kind; love is not envious or boastful or arrogant or rude. It does not insist on its own way; it is not irritable or resentful; it does not rejoice in wrongdoing, but rejoices in the truth. It bears all things, believes all things, hopes all things, endures all things.

Love never ends. But as for prophecies, they will come to an end; as for tongues, they will cease; as for knowledge, it will come to an end.

Love never ends.

The Word of the Lord

Reflection

(please adapt this reflection as necessary to suit the gender of N)

We are gathered to celebrate the life God gave to N, to thank God for giving him to us and to pray that he will enjoy eternal life with God in heaven. Some of you are people of faith; some belong to different faith communities; some are people who once had a faith but no longer believe.

We all knew N in different ways. To his wife he was a loving husband; to his children he was a devoted father; to others of you he was a brother. Some of you knew him as a friend or work colleague or maybe you played football or golf with him. Maybe you enjoyed a pint with him or sang with him or even laughed at his jokes! Yes, we all knew him in different ways. But the one uniting factor in the midst of all our sorrow is love. We each loved him in our own different way.

The piece from Paul's letter to the Corinthians that we have just heard read for us is normally associated with wedding ceremonies. So why has it been chosen for this funeral service today? Well, it speaks of that love that unites us. A friend of mine, Colin Parkes, once wrote, 'The pain of grief is just as much part of life as the joy of love; it is perhaps the price we pay for love, the cost of commitment.' [10] *Love, life and grief are inextricably linked.*

Paul gives us a very comprehensive description of what love is – patience, kindness, trust, hope. It is never rude, conceited or boastful. But the greatest quality of love that Paul speaks of is that it 'does not come to an end'. Today we grieve, we hurt, we are sad, and rightly so. This man whom we loved, who shared our life, has died, and over the coming days, weeks, months and even longer we will continue to feel grief. But hopefully we can find some comfort in those words, 'Love never ends.' For as much as we know N has died, we also know that the love between him and you hasn't died. N is no longer physically alive with us but the love you shared transcends even death itself. It will never die. As Dylan Thomas

10   Colin Murray Parkes, *Bereavement: Studies of Grief in Adult Life* (London: Penguin, 1975).

once wrote, 'Though lovers be lost, love shall not.'

The first letter of St John says, 'Let us love one another, because love is from God; everyone who loves is born of God and knows God. Whoever does not love does not know God, for God is love' (1 John 4:7–8). There is a divine quality to love. We are united in God for all eternity and we are united in love. This is the hope that we share through faith and St Paul concludes this chapter of his letter with that beautiful sentence, 'In short, there are three things that last; faith, hope and love; and the greatest of these is love.'

John O'Donohue put it nicely in his poem/prayer, 'For Lost Friends',

> *May we have the grace to see*
> *Despite the hurt of rapture*
> *The searing of anger*
> *And the empty disappointment,*
> *That whoever we have loved,*
> *Such love can never quench.*[11]

A Reading from the Letter of St Paul to the Philippians (3:20–21)

But our citizenship is in heaven, and it is from there that we are expecting a Savior, the Lord Jesus Christ. He will transform the body of our humiliation that it may be conformed to the body of his glory, by the power that also enables him to make all things subject to himself.

The Word of the Lord

Reflection

This is a short yet rich reading from Paul. Two aspects of what he says strike me. The first is Paul's assertion that our homeland is in heaven. Paul was very aware of his Roman citizenship and the

11   John O'Donohue, 'For Lost Friends', *Benedictus* (London: Bantam Press, 2007).

benefits and rights it conferred on him. Here he reminds us that by virtue of our relationship with Christ we have a much greater citizenship – heaven is our homeland; we are citizens of heaven with all the benefits that bestows on us. First and foremost is our sharing in the transfigured glorious body of Christ. And that leads to the second point that strikes me.

There is an account in St John's Gospel (20:15) of how Mary Magdalene encounters the risen Christ after his resurrection on that first Easter Sunday. At first she didn't recognise him – even when he spoke to her. John tells us that she supposed him to be the gardener. Something about Jesus' appearance had obviously changed to such an extent that Mary initially didn't recognise him. He had been transformed. The Gospels of Matthew, Mark and Luke all describe an event known as the Transfiguration, when Jesus took Peter, James and John with him up Mount Tabor where they witnessed a vision of Jesus transfigured in glory – a foretaste of the glory of the Risen Christ.

St Paul tells us in this reading that after our death we too will go through a 'transformation' of our own. The Lord Jesus will transform our bodies into copies of his own glorious body. We will have no need of the body we lived in here on earth. Because we share in Christ's resurrection, we share in his glorious body.

In his book Anam Chara, *John O'Donohue recounts how a son of one of his friends had died and as she stood at his graveside with her other children, a terrible wail of sadness went up from them. Putting her arms around them she said, 'Ná bígí ag caoineadh, níl tada dhó thios ansin ach amháin an clúdach a bhí air.' (Don't be crying. There is nothing of him down there, only the covering that was on him in this life.) She recognised that our earthly body is 'merely a covering and the soul is now freed for the eternal'.* [12]

---

12 John O'Donohue, *Anam Chara* (London: Bantam Press, 1997).

A Reading from the First Letter of St Paul to the Thessalonians (4:13–18)

But we do not want you to be uninformed, brothers and sisters, about those who have died, so that you may not grieve as others do who have no hope. For since we believe that Jesus died and rose again, even so, through Jesus, God will bring with him those who have died. For this we declare to you by the word of the Lord, that we who are alive, who are left until the coming of the Lord, will by no means precede those who have died. For the Lord himself, with a cry of command, with the archangel's call and with the sound of God's trumpet, will descend from heaven, and the dead in Christ will rise first. Then we who are alive, who are left, will be caught up in the clouds together with them to meet the Lord in the air; and so we will be with the Lord forever. Therefore encourage one another with these words.

The Word of the Lord

Reflection

On first look we'd be forgiven for thinking St Paul is telling us here, that as Christians we should not be grieving. However, what he is saying is that, yes, absolutely, we grieve, but we do so as people of hope, unlike those who have no hope.

Paul then goes on to describe that hope that we have. It comes from our faith; from our belief in the resurrection. When Jesus rose from the dead he conquered death. Death will have no more power over us. We too will rise to be with God in heaven. It's the same hope that Jesus told us of in John's Gospel when he promised, 'I will come again and will take you to myself, so that where I am, there you may be also' (John 14:3).

I often think that it must be incredibly heart-breaking to believe that nothing exists beyond the here and now; that at the end of my life I will simply cease to exist. If this life is all there is, then surely its ending produces tremendous grief. But that is not the case for followers of Christ, says Paul. Life after death, that life with Our Father in heaven, is central to our Christian belief. And that is what differentiates the grieving of Christians from a grief that lacks that hope and trust in God's promise. It is what Jesus told his followers in Mark's Gospel:

Then they will see 'the Son of Man coming in clouds' with great power and glory. Then he will send out the angels, and gather his elect from the four winds, from the ends of the earth to the ends of heaven. (Mark 13:26–27)

Paul concludes this part of his letter by telling his listeners to encourage one another with thoughts such as these. So, as we gather today and face the future grieving our loss we can encourage and comfort one another, as we shall hear in our prayers later at the graveside, 'in sure and certain hope of the resurrection to eternal life through our Lord Jesus Christ'.

A Reading from the First Letter of St John (3:1–2)

See what love the Father has given us, that we should be called children of God; and that is what we are. The reason the world does not know us is that it did not know him. Beloved, we are God's children now; what we will be has not yet been revealed. What we do know is this: when he is revealed, we will be like him, for we will see him as he is.

The Word of the Lord

Reflection
God's love is freely given to us. It's not something we have earned. And what is it that he has bestowed on us? We are to be called his

children. Those words 'be called' are important. We are what we are called. The name 'Christian' was first given to followers of Jesus in the early days of the Church in Antioch. And to this day we are called Christians. We belong to Christ. Central to our faith is that Jesus Christ, whose name means the saviour, the rescuer, the anointed one, is the Son of God. And we have been freely given sonship or daughtership of God. A friend of mine who was adopted said that he felt extremely honoured and loved by the free choice of his adoptive parents to call him their son. It was not something he had earned as of right.

In the Church we become children of God when we are baptised. N was baptised on (date) and became a child of God and a member of the Christian family. At various times throughout life we recall our baptism and today is no exception. As N's body was brought into the Church for his/her funeral he/she was sprinkled with holy water as a reminder of his/her baptism and before we leave the church today to take him/her to his/her place of rest we will repeat that memorial.

An aspect of being someone's child is what we inherit from that person. We are all familiar with the doting relatives cooing over a newborn baby and saying, 'He has his father's eyes', or 'He has his mother's nose', or 'Isn't he the image of our ones!' We inherit not just looks, but also beliefs and personality traits. How many people have we heard talking and thought they sound just like their father – not just their accent but in how they phrase things or in the thoughts they are expressing. I believe that one of the most important things that we can inherit is faith.

So, as children of faith, as children of God, what do we inherit? John tells us, 'We will be like him, for we will see him as he is.' The promise made to us is that we will share in Jesus' resurrection and have eternal life with him. As Christ promised in John's Gospel, he has gone ahead to prepare a place for us so that where he is, we too may be. That is our inheritance; to be with Christ our brother, in the presence of our heavenly Father, for ever. We are also told

97

in John's Gospel that God is love. In heaven we will find ourselves in the presence of a love so perfect, that it is immeasurably greater than any love we have known here on earth.

And our prayer today is that N is now enjoying his/her heavenly inheritance and that one day we too will enjoy that inheritance with him/her and with all those who have gone before us.

SOME GOSPEL READINGS

A Reading from the Holy Gospel According to Matthew (5:1–12)

When Jesus saw the crowds, he went up the mountain; and after he sat down, his disciples came to him. Then he began to speak, and taught them, saying:
'Blessed are the poor in spirit, for theirs is the kingdom of heaven.
'Blessed are those who mourn, for they will be comforted.
'Blessed are the meek, for they will inherit the earth.
'Blessed are those who hunger and thirst for righteousness, for they will be filled.
'Blessed are the merciful, for they will receive mercy.
'Blessed are the pure in heart, for they will see God.
'Blessed are the peacemakers, for they will be called children of God.
'Blessed are those who are persecuted for righteousness' sake, for theirs is the kingdom of heaven.
'Blessed are you when people revile you and persecute you and utter all kinds of evil against you falsely on my account. Rejoice and be glad, for your reward is great in heaven, for in the same way they persecuted the prophets who were before you.

The Gospel of the Lord

Reflection

This passage from Matthew's Gospel is known as the Beatitudes. Pope Francis has described it as a roadmap for Christian life. It seems to turn logic on its head. How can the poor in spirit be happy or blessed? How can we be happy in our mourning? How are we happy or blessed if we are yearning for right and justice? And what's all this about being blessed by being persecuted?

St Paul addressed this in his first letter to the Corinthians when he said, 'For God's foolishness is wiser than human wisdom, and God's weakness is stronger than human strength. But God chose what is foolish in the world to shame the wise; God chose what is weak in the world to shame the strong' (1 Corinthians 1:25, 27). We live in a world where meekness is viewed as weakness. We have to be ambitious; we have to get to the top of the pile, whether that be at work or in sports, for example, even if it means stepping on others to get there. But Jesus is telling us that the blessed thing, the thing that leads to true happiness, is to be meek.

If we read through the Beatitudes they present us with many situations in life where we can be blessed or where we can bless others. We can be happy and blessed when we are gentle; when we are merciful; when we are peacemakers. We can be a blessing for others when we challenge poverty; when we challenge lack of justice; when we challenge persecution.

What concerns us most today, of course, is the one that says, 'Happy are those who mourn.' As you mourn the death of N, I'm sure you feel anything but blessed. Grief can leave us broken-hearted and feeling empty. There is an old saying in Irish, 'Tá an cupán folamh ann le líonadh' – the empty cup is there to be filled. The emptiness you feel can be filled; you can be comforted, even though it may not feel like it now. The prayers and readings we share with you today will hopefully bring some solace. Perhaps the empty cup will be filled by the people who came to the house to support you; the people gathered around you today.

Some time ago I wrote a poem called 'Death Where Is Thy

Sting?' In it I asked 'Death, where is thy consolation?' The response includes the lines,

> *It is in the presence of you and*
> *In the healing silence.*
> *It's in your prayerful presence and*
> *Loving embrace.*

I pray that, today and in the days to come, you will feel the presence and loving embrace of your friends.

In this Beatitude the other side of the coin is that we, as a community, are challenged to comfort those mourn. Not in Facebook 'thoughts and prayers' or in pious platitudes, but in our prayerful presence and loving embrace.

So, we pray that you who mourn will be blessed and the rest of us will there to bless you.

A Reading from the Holy Gospel According to Mark (15:33–39)

When it was noon, darkness came over the whole land until three in the afternoon. At three o'clock Jesus cried out with a loud voice, *'Eloi, Eloi, lema sabachthani?'* which means, 'My God, my God, why have you forsaken me?' When some of the bystanders heard it, they said, 'Listen, he is calling for Elijah.' And someone ran, filled a sponge with sour wine, put it on a stick, and gave it to him to drink, saying, 'Wait, let us see whether Elijah will come to take him down.' Then Jesus gave a loud cry and breathed his last. And the curtain of the temple was torn in two, from top to bottom. Now when the centurion, who stood facing him, saw that in this way he breathed his last, he said, 'Truly this man was God's Son!'

The Gospel of the Lord

Reflection

There are three particular sentences that speak to me in this passage today.

The first is, 'My God, my God, why have you forsaken me?' It is a cry that many of us could make, especially in the midst of grief. But where is God now? It is easy to feel that we have been deserted, or forsaken, by God. We have been taught that God is love; that God is always there when we are in pain. Often when a grieving person meets someone else who has endured a similar bereavement, the other person will say something like, 'I know exactly what you are going through'. The reality is that they don't. They can't. All they know is what they felt in similar circumstances. Here, while Jesus is not experiencing exactly what we are, Mark is telling us that he has that similar feeling of being forsaken by God, his Father. I find that comforting. Jesus has been there before me and if he had that feeling, then it's okay for me to feel that way.

The second sentence that strikes me is, 'Jesus gave a loud cry and breathed his last.' What was in that cry of anguish and grief? I believe that Jesus was crying out for all of us. He was taking all of our pain into his own body. Our tears became his tears. He was crying out for everyone humiliated; everyone who has been treated unjustly; for every widow and widower; for every parent who has held their dead or dying child; for every human person bereaved or suffering in whatever way. He is crying for me when I can't cry any more.

The third sentence is the very last one, spoken by the centurion at the foot of the cross. 'Truly this man was God's son.' Some of you may remember the film The Greatest Story Ever Told. *The crucifixion scene was based largely on Mark's account and the actor chosen to speak that line was John Wayne. Now Wayne was a famous actor, having appeared in many, many films, and yet these were his only words in this film; this was his only scene. I wonder if there was a reason why such a famous actor was cast in this role? Was it because of the importance of the sentence? Perhaps not, but I like to think that perhaps it might have been. The centurion was bearing witness to Christ as God's son. Having witnessed Jesus' humanity in his suffering, he was now bearing witness to his divinity. Because we share in the sonship of Christ we all can be called sons or daughters of God. And today we say that of N. By virtue of his/her baptism and God's saving grace he/she is a son/daughter of God. And because we are children of God, we share in the same inheritance as Jesus. Even as we share in pain and grief, we share in his resurrection and in his eternal life in heaven with God our Father.*

A Reading from the Holy Gospel According to Luke (24:13–16, 27–35)

Now on that same day two of them were going to a village called Emmaus, about seven miles from Jerusalem, and talking with each other about all these things that had happened. While they were talking and discussing, Jesus himself came near and went with them, but their eyes were kept from recognizing him.

Then beginning with Moses and all the prophets, he interpreted to them the things about himself in all the scriptures.

As they came near the village to which they were going, he walked ahead as if he were going on. But they urged him strongly, saying, 'Stay with us, because it is almost evening and the day is now nearly over.' So he went in to stay with them. When he was at the table with them, he took bread, blessed and broke it, and gave it to them. Then their eyes were opened, and they recognized him; and he vanished from their sight. They said to each other, 'Were not our hearts burning within us while he was talking to us on the road, while he was opening the scriptures to us?' That same hour they got up and returned to Jerusalem;

and they found the eleven and their companions gathered together. They were saying, 'The Lord has risen indeed, and he has appeared to Simon!' Then they told what had happened on the road, and how he had been made known to them in the breaking of the bread. *The Gospel of the Lord*

Reflection

In celebrating the funeral Mass for N, we come together, as we do at every Mass, to be nourished by the word of God and by his body and blood in the Eucharist, just as the two disciples were in their encounter with the risen Christ in this gospel passage. Participation in the Mass, availing of that nourishment, was a regular feature of N's life and it is fitting that we too come to be so nourished as we pray for the happy repose of his/her soul and for consolation in our grief.

We listen to God's word in the Scriptures, hearing what prophets, disciples and Christ himself had to say about God's relationship with us; of how he spoke to his people through the generations right up to when he sent his only beloved son, his Word made flesh, to walk among us. We hear how Christ died on the cross for our sins and, most importantly, how he rose from the dead, conquering death and sin and giving us the promise of a share in that resurrection.

Having listened to and been nourished by the word of God, we then share in the breaking of bread where Jesus makes himself present among us again, as he did with the two disciples in Emmaus. We are told that when Jesus blessed and broke the bread their eyes were opened, and they recognised Jesus there with them. He is present here today in our midst as we celebrate the funeral rites for N.

So, we pray that N will see the fulfilment of that promise of a share in Jesus' resurrection and victory over death. We also pray that not only our eyes, but our hearts too will be open to seeing Christ present with us to give us his consolation. As St Paul said in his second letter to the Corinthians, 'through Christ does our consolation overflow' (2 Corinthians 1:5).

A Reading from the Holy Gospel According to John (11:32–45)

When Mary came where Jesus was and saw him, she knelt at his feet and said to him, 'Lord, if you had been here, my brother would not have died.' When Jesus saw her weeping, and the Jews who came with her also weeping, he was greatly disturbed in spirit and deeply moved. He said, 'Where have you laid him?' They said to him, 'Lord, come and see.' Jesus wept. So the Jews said, 'See how he loved him!' But some of them said, 'Could not he who opened the eyes of the blind man have kept this man from dying?'

Then Jesus, again greatly disturbed, came to the tomb. It was a cave, and a stone was lying against it. Jesus said, 'Take away the stone.' Martha, the sister of the dead man, said to him, 'Lord, already there is a stench because he has been dead four days.' Jesus said to her, 'Did I not tell you that if you believed, you would see the glory of God?' So they took away the stone. And Jesus looked upward and said, 'Father, I thank you for having heard me. I knew that you always hear me, but I have said this for the sake of the crowd standing here, so that they may believe that you sent me.' When he had said this, he cried with a loud voice, 'Lazarus, come out!' The dead man came out, his hands and feet bound with strips of cloth, and his face wrapped in a cloth. Jesus said to them, 'Unbind him, and let him go.'

Many of the Jews therefore, who had come with Mary and had seen what Jesus did, believed in him.

The Gospel of the Lord

Reflection

Some years ago, I was invited to a girls' secondary school in West Belfast. I was asked to lead a session on loss and grief with a sixth-form RE class. I selected this passage from John's Gospel and, after having read it, I invited the girls to act out the story. I told them to imagine what it was like that day. When Lazarus was taken ill, Martha and Mary had sent for Jesus, but by the time he got there Lazarus was already dead and buried. How did they feel? How did they react to Jesus when he arrived? I told them to try to put themselves in the minds of Martha and Mary and their friends. I also told them to speak exactly how they felt, and not to hold back! They didn't hold back! When the girl playing the role of Jesus came in, the two acting Martha and Mary 'laid into him'. 'Jesus, where were you?' 'What the **** kept you?' 'If you'd been here he wouldn't have died!' They really got into their roles, language and all! After the roleplay we sat around and discussed the various emotions they thought Lazarus's sisters and their friends would have been experiencing. Yes, they talked about all the usual ones – sorrow, sadness, guilt, but high among them was anger at Jesus. We went on to discuss feeling angry at God, at Jesus. Was it normal? Was it allowed? I assured them it was perfectly natural and certainly allowed.

An elderly woman I used to visit said to me one time, 'God and me's the best of friends but sometimes I fall out with him. But sure, we always make up again.' It is both natural and allowable to feel angry at God and to express it. That's what prayer is for – to lay our thoughts and feelings before God.

Some of you today may be feeling angry at God. Tell him! When my mother died I felt like that. Why did God allow her to die when lots of bad/evil people were allowed to live and prosper? I didn't really get an answer. I came to learn to live without one as I came to learn to live without my mother.

What I do know is that whatever I feel, however I grieve, Jesus has been there too. We hear in this gospel that he was in great

105

distress; that he spoke 'with a sigh that came straight from the heart'. And in that shortest of verses in all of Scripture, 'Jesus wept'. I also know that if Jesus has shared in our grief, we will also share in his glory. We will hear the words spoken by Jesus at the end of this gospel reading, 'Unbind him, and let him go.' And it is the same for everyone in this congregation and it is the same for N, whom we mourn today. Through Christ he/she will be unbound and set free.

A Reading from the Holy Gospel According to John (12:23–26)

Jesus answered them, 'The hour has come for the Son of Man to be glorified. Very truly, I tell you, unless a grain of wheat falls into the earth and dies, it remains just a single grain; but if it dies, it bears much fruit. Those who love their life lose it, and those who hate their life in this world will keep it for eternal life. Whoever serves me must follow me, and where I am, there will my servant be also. Whoever serves me, the Father will honor.

The Gospel of the Lord

Reflection

This short reading tells of Jesus' words to his disciples as he wound down his earthly ministry and prepared for his death on the cross and his resurrection. He uses the imagery of the grain of wheat, sown and dying in order to produce a rich harvest. Jesus spoke frequently about the dichotomy of good and evil, light and dark, life and death. Here he is comparing the death of the grain of wheat with the new life of the harvest, with his own death and resurrection, and, in turn, with our losing our earthly life but gaining eternal life with Christ.

Nature is rich in examples of this kind of death versus life imagery. Apart from the image of the grain of wheat dying to yield the harvest, you will be aware of the saying, 'Great oaks out of little acorns grow'. You will also be aware of the imagery of the caterpillar that transforms into a beautiful butterfly. This is a particularly interesting comparison. The second part of the word caterpillar has its roots in the old French word piller, meaning to plunder. In the Old Testament caterpillars were included in the plagues of Egypt because of their association with locusts. If you've ever tried to grow lettuce you'll know what happens when the caterpillars get at them! Yet, in spite of this negative image of the plundering caterpillar, when the caterpillar ceases to be, it transforms into a beautiful butterfly. Butterflies are an entirely different proposition from caterpillars. Richard Bach wrote, 'What the caterpillar calls the end of the world, the Master calls a butterfly.' And so, it is for us. At the end of our existence here on earth we are called to be transformed into something new and beautiful. It won't exactly be a butterfly, but as we read in the first letter of St John, 'What we will has not yet been revealed. What we do know is this: when he is revealed, we will be like him, for we will see him as he is' (1 John 3:2).

A Reading from the Holy Gospel According to John (20:11–18)

But Mary stood weeping outside the tomb. As she wept, she bent over to look into the tomb; and she saw two angels in white, sitting where the body of Jesus had been lying, one at the head and the other at the feet. They said to her, 'Woman, why are you weeping?' She said to them, 'They have taken away my Lord, and I do not know where they have laid him.' When she had said this, she turned around and saw Jesus standing there, but she did not know that it was Jesus. Jesus said to her, 'Woman, why are you weeping? Whom are you looking for?' Supposing him to be the gardener, she said to him, 'Sir, if you have carried him away, tell me where you have laid him, and I will take him away.' Jesus said to her, 'Mary!' She turned and said to him in Hebrew, 'Rabbouni!' (which means Teacher). Jesus said to her, 'Do not hold on to me, because I have not yet ascended to the Father. But go to my brothers and say to them, "I am ascending to my Father and your Father, to my God and your God."' Mary Magdalene went and announced to the disciples, 'I have seen the Lord'; and she told them that he had said these things to her.

The Gospel of the Lord

Reflection

Three things speak to me in this account from John's Gospel.

Firstly, we read how Mary of Magdala was searching for her friend Jesus who had died just a few days previously. This is, of course, one of the very natural reactions to death. We search for the one we have lost. By going to the tomb and looking around, this is just what Mary was doing, even to the extent of asking these two men if they had seen him. Then she spotted a stranger whom she supposed to be the gardener and virtually accused him of taking Jesus away. There is a message for us here. What we are experiencing in our grief is nothing new. It is as natural as breathing. It's what humans do when someone close to them dies.

Secondly, Mary mistook Jesus for the gardener. She didn't think he was a rabbi, or a priest or a theologian. No, she supposed him to be the gardener. In some ways a gardener is indeed a very apt description of Jesus. What does a gardener do? He plants seeds; he nurtures them, feeding and watering them till they grow into healthy plants; he prunes them, sometimes cutting them right back, to bring them to maturity. That's what Jesus does for us. He plants the seed of faith within us. You'll be familiar with the parable of the sower in the gospels. In other parts of his teaching

108

Jesus uses that comparison with gardening, comparing himself, for instance, to the vinedresser. Earlier in John's Gospel he tells us that unless a grain of wheat falls to the ground and dies, it remains only a single grain; but if it dies it yields a rich harvest (John 12:24). This is key to Christ's teaching about himself and his resurrection. Life springs from death. Jesus had to die to rise again to new life. Each of us has to die in order to inherit eternal life.

Thirdly, Jesus called Mary by her name. He said to her, 'Mary', and she knew him, and said to him in Hebrew, 'Rabbuni'. We are all called by name. In Isaiah, God tells us through the prophet, 'Do not be afraid, for I have redeemed you; I have called you by your name, you are mine' (Isaiah 43:2). When we were baptised the priest asked our parents, 'What name do you give your child?' When our life on earth comes to an end we are called by name. We have been redeemed and belong to God. That is what we celebrate today for N. He/she has been called by name and redeemed. His/her new life springs from his/her death. He/she belongs to God and with God.

SAMPLE PRAYERS OF INTERCESSION

The prayers of intercession take place after the homily and are introduced and concluded by the celebrant. The individual intercessions may be delivered by members of the deceased's family circle, by parish ministers of the word or by the celebrant. The following are examples of prayers that might be used and could be adapted or indeed replaced by others more suitable for individual needs. It is usual to have between four and six intercessions.

Celebrant (Introduction):
We pray now for our brother/sister who has died. We pray also for ourselves in our grief and for all our needs.

Or

Confident in Christ's promise, 'Ask and you shall receive', we now place our needs before him and pray.

Or

God the almighty Father raised Jesus from the dead. With confidence we pray for N and all our deceased who have gone before us marked with the sign of faith. We pray also for the needs of our families, our own parish community and wider society.

Or

God, the Father almighty, raised Jesus from the dead and he will give life to our own mortal bodies. We pray to him in faith.

Reader/s (Intercessions):

In baptism N was given the pledge of eternal life. May she/he be admitted now to the company of saints in heaven. Lord hear us.

Response: Lord graciously hear us.

For N: that God may have mercy on his/her soul and grant him/her eternal rest. Lord hear us. **R**

We thank you for all the blessings and joy you gave N in this life. May she/he enjoy them a hundredfold in your eternal kingdom. Lord hear us. **R**

For (name other relatives who have died) who have gone before us and for all the faithful departed that they may rest in peace. Lord hear us. **R**

May N's strong, steadfast and yet simple faith be a source of inspiration to us all. Lord hear us. **R**

For all here present and for all who mourn for N. Give us your consolation and strength in these dark days and in the days to come. Sustain us with the faith that one day we will all be reunited in your kingdom. Lord hear us. **R**

For all here present, that Christ our Lord may open our hearts to receive his love and the good news of salvation. Lord hear us. **R**

We pray that the Lord will be with us on the road of life; let us feel his strength in our weakness, his light in times of darkness of spirit and his comforting presence in times of distress. Lord hear us. **R**

For all those suffering throughout the world from hunger or disease or from the evils of war. Let them know your love and care for them in the midst of their pain. Lord hear us. **R**

Many people die by violence, war and famine each day. Show your mercy to all those who suffer from injustice and from sins against your love. Gather them into your eternal kingdom of peace. Lord hear us. **R**

We remember those who have died at a young age and those who have died as a result of suicide or violence. Give them eternal rest and peace and console those who grieve for them. Lord hear us. **R**

For all doctors, nurses and carers, especially those who looked after N in his/her last days. May they continue to have kind hearts and gentle hands. Lord hear us. **R**

For those who attended to N's spiritual welfare (e.g. priests, eucharistic ministers, hospital chaplaincy team etc.). May God give them strength to continue in their good work. Lord hear us. **R**

Celebrant (Conclusion):

Father, into your hands we commend our brother/sister N. We ask you to look gently upon him/her and upon us as we make these, our prayers, to you in faith, through Christ, our Lord. Amen.

Or

God, Father almighty, our shelter and our strength, listen in love to the cry of your people and hear these prayers that we make to you through Christ, our Lord. Amen.

Or

Lord God, giver of peace and healer of souls, listen to our prayers for N, for ourselves and for all your people. Be attentive to our needs and answer this prayer that we make to you through Christ, our Lord. Amen.

Or

God of the living and of the dead, you brought Jesus back to life; raise up the faithful departed, and let us come with them into your heavenly glory, through Christ our Lord. Amen.

APPENDIX:
PROSE EXTRACTS, POEMS AND PRAYERS

PROSE

The Price we Pay for Love
(Colin Murray Parkes, *Bereavement*, London: Penguin 1975)

Just as broken bones may end up stronger than unbroken ones, so the experience of grieving can strengthen and bring maturity to those who have been previously protected from misfortune. The pain of grief is just as much a part of life as the joy of love; it is, perhaps, the price we pay for love, the cost of commitment. To ignore this fact, or to pretend that it is not so, is to put on emotional blinkers which leave us unprepared for the losses that will inevitably occur in our lives and unprepared to help others to cope with the losses in theirs.

All Is Well
(Henry Scott Holland, from verses 4–5 of the hymn 'Grant Us Thy Light', adapted)

Death is nothing at all … I have only slipped away into the next room. I am I and you are you. Whatever we were to each other, that we are still. Call me by my old familiar name, speak to me in the easy way which you always used. Put no difference in your tone; wear no forced air of solemnity or sorrow. Laugh as we always laughed at the little jokes we enjoyed together. Play, smile, think of me, pray for me. Let my name be always the household word that it always was. Let it be spoken without effort, without the ghost of a shadow on it. Life means all it ever meant. It is the same as it ever was; there is absolutely unbroken continuity. Why should I be out of mind because I am out of sight? I am waiting for you for an interval, somewhere very near, just around the corner. All is well.

Something Incredible
(Oscar Wilde, *De Profundis*)

There is still something to me almost incredible in the idea of a young Galilean peasant imagining that he could bear on his own shoulders the burden of the entire world; all that had already been done and suffered, and all that was yet to be done and suffered: the sins of Nero, of Caesar Borgia, of Alexander VI, and of him who was Emperor of Rome and Priest of the Sun: the sufferings of those whose names are legion and whose dwelling is among the tombs: oppressed nationalities, factory children, thieves, people in prison, outcasts, those who are dumb under oppression and whose silence is heard only of God; and not merely imagining this but actually achieving it, so that at the present moment all who come into contact with his personality, even though they may neither bow to his altar nor kneel before his priest, in some way find that the ugliness of their sin is taken away and the beauty of their sorrow revealed to them.

POEMS

Am Always With You
(Anon)

When I am gone, release me, let me go.
I have so many things to see and do,
You mustn't tie yourself to me with too many tears,
But be thankful we had so many good years.
I gave you my love, and you can only guess
How much you've given me in happiness.
I thank you for the love that you have shown,
But now it is time I travelled on alone.
So grieve for me a while, if grieve you must
Then let your grief be comforted by trust
That it is only for a while that we must part,

So treasure the memories within your heart.
I won't be far away for life goes on.
And if you need me, call and I will come.
Though you can't see or touch me, I will be near
And if you listen with your heart, you'll hear
All my love around you soft and clear
And then, when you come this way alone,
I'll greet you with a smile and a 'Welcome Home'.

Solitary Man
(Laurence McKeown, *Threads*, Ennistymon: Salmon Poetry, 2018)

Comrade,
why do you weep unseen?
Why speak fears to yourself
and create echoes of a darker you?

We laugh with one another;
why can't we cry together?

I See His Blood upon the Rose
(Joseph Mary Plunkett)

I see his blood upon the rose
And in the stars the glory of his eyes,
His body gleams amid eternal snows,
His tears fall from the skies.

I see his face in every flower;
The thunder and the singing of the birds
Are but his voice – and carven by his power
Rocks are his written words.

All pathways by his feet are worn,
His strong heart stirs the ever-beating sea,

His crown of thorns is twined with every thorn,
His cross is every tree.

No Man is an Island
(John Donne)

No man is an island entire of itself; every man
is a piece of the continent, a part of the main;
if a clod be washed away by the sea, Europe
is the less, as well as is if a promontory were, as
well as any manner of thy friends or of thine
own were; any man's death diminishes me,
because I am involved in mankind.
And therefore never send to know for whom
the bell tolls; it tolls for thee.

Death where is thy Sting
(Paddy Shannon, 2020)

Death where is thy sting?
Let me tell you.
It's in my breaking heart
within my aching breast.
It's in my heartfelt fear and
In my river of tears.
It's in the heat of my anger and
In the burden of my guilt.

But death where is thy consolation?
It's not in the Facebook thoughts and prayers nor
In the pious platitudes of
A better place and God's beautiful garden.
It is in the presence of you and
In the healing silence
It's in your prayerful presence and

Loving embrace.
It's in the God man Jesus
Who wept for Lazarus
And called him forth;
It's in the enduring love of the risen Christ
Who went ahead
To show us the way, the truth and the life
So that where he is
We too may be.

For Life and Death are One
(Khalil Gibran, *The Prophet*, London: Heinemann, 1926)

You would know the secret of death,
But how shall you find it unless you seek it in the heart of life?
The owl, whose night-bound eyes are blind unto the day,
cannot unveil the mystery of light.
If you would indeed behold the spirit of death,
open up your heart wide into the body of life,
For life and death are one, even as the river and the sea are one.

Fear
(Khalil Gibran, ibid.)

It is said before entering the sea
a river trembles with fear.

She looks back at the path she has travelled,
from the peaks of the mountains,
the long winding road crossing forests and villages.

And in front of her,
she sees an ocean so vast,
that to enter
there seems nothing more than to disappear forever.

But there is no other way.
The river cannot go back.

Nobody can go back.
To go back is impossible in existence.

The river needs to take the risk
of entering the ocean
because only then will fear disappear,
because that's where the river will know
it's not about disappearing into the ocean,
but of becoming the ocean.

The Ship

(Henry Van Dyke, nineteenth-century clergyman, educator, poet and religious writer)

I am standing upon the seashore.
A ship at my side spreads her white
sails to the morning breeze and starts
for the blue ocean.
She is an object of beauty and strength.
I stand and watch her until at length
she hangs like a speck of white cloud
just where the sea and sky come
to mingle with each other.
Then, someone at my side says;
'There, she is gone!'
'Gone where?'
Gone from my sight. That is all.
She is just as large in mast and hull
and spar as she was when she left my side
and she is just as able to bear her
load of living freight to her destined port.
Her diminished size is in me, not in her.

And just at the moment when someone
at my side says, 'There, she is gone!'
There are other eyes watching her coming,
and other voices ready to take up the glad
shout;
'Here she comes!'
And that is dying.

Afterglow
(Anon)

I'd like the memory of me
To be a happy one.
I'd like to leave an afterglow
Of smiles when life is done.
I'd like to leave an echo
Whispering softly down the ways,
Of happy times and laughing times
And bright and sunny days.
I'd like the tears of those who grieve
To dry before the sun
Of happy memories
That I leave when life is done.

The Cord
(Anon)

We are connected,
My child and I, by
An invisible cord
Not seen by the eye.
It's not like the cord
That connects us 'til birth,
This cord can't be seen
by any on earth.

This cord does its work
Right from the start
It binds us together,
Attached to my heart.
I know it's there
Though no one can see
The invisible cord
From my child to me.
The strength of this cord
Is hard to describe.
It can't be destroyed
It can't be denied.
It's a cord much stronger than
Man could create
It withstands the test,
Can hold my weight.
And though you are gone,
And you're not here with me,
The cord is still there
But no one can see.
It pulls at my heart,
I am bruised … I am sore,

But this cord is my lifeline
As never before.
I am thankful that God
Connects us this way.
A mother and child
Death can't take away!

On the Death of the Beloved
(John O'Donohue, *Benedictus*, London: Bantam Press, 2007)

Though we need to weep your loss,
You dwell in that safe place in our hearts,

Where no storm or night or pain can reach you.

Your love was like the dawn
Brightening over our lives,
Awakening beneath the dark
A further adventure of colour.
The sound of your voice
Found for us
A new music
That brightened everything.
Whatever you enfolded in your gaze
Quickened in the joy of its being;
You placed smiles like flowers
On the altar of the heart.
Your mind always sparkled
With wonder at things.

Though your days here were brief,
Your spirit was alive, awake, complete.

We look towards each other no longer
From the old distance of our names;
Now you dwell inside the rhythm of breath,
As close to us as we are to ourselves.

Though we cannot see you with outward eyes,
We know our soul's gaze is upon your face,
Smiling back at us from within everything
To which we bring our best refinement.

Let us not look for you only in memory,
Where we would grow lonely without you.
You would want us to find you in presence,
Beside us when beauty brightens,
When kindness glows

And music echoes eternal tones.

When orchids brighten the earth,
Darkest winter has turned to spring;
May this dark grief flower with hope
In every heart that loves you.

May you continue to inspire us:

To enter each day with a generous heart.
To serve the call of courage and love
Until we see your beautiful face again
In that land where there is no more separation,
Where all tears will be wiped from our mind,
And where we will never lose you again.

For Grief
(John O'Donohue, ibid.)

When you lose someone you love,
Your life becomes strange,
The ground beneath you becomes fragile,
Your thoughts make your eyes unsure;
And some dead echo drags your voice down
Where words have no confidence.

Your heart has grown heavy with loss;
And though this loss has wounded others too,
No one knows what has been taken from you
When the silence of absence deepens.

Flickers of guilt kindle regret
For all that was left unsaid or undone.
There are days when you wake up happy;
Again inside the fullness of life,

122

Until the moment breaks
And you are thrown back
Onto the black tide of loss.

Days when you have your heart back,
You are able to function well
Until in the middle of work or encounter,
Suddenly with no warning,
You are ambushed by grief.
It becomes hard to trust yourself.
All you can depend on now is that
Sorrow will remain faithful to itself.

More than you, it knows its way
And will find the right time
To pull and pull the rope of grief
Until that coiled hill of tears
Has reduced to its last drop.

Gradually you will learn acquaintance
With the invisible form of your departed;
And when the work of grief is done,
The wound of loss will heal
And you will have learned
To wean your eyes
From that gap in the air
And be able to enter the hearth
In your soul where your loved one
Has awaited your return
All the time.

Requiescat
(Written by twelve-year-old Oscar Wilde after the death of his nine-year-old sister Isola)

Tread lightly, she is near
Under the snow,
Speak gently, she can hear
The daisies grow.

All her bright golden hair
Tarnished with rust,
She that was young and fair
Fallen to dust.
Lily-like, white as snow,
She hardly knew
She was a woman, so
Sweetly she grew.

Coffin-board, heavy stone,
Lie on her breast,
I vex my heart alone
She is at rest.

Peace, Peace, she cannot hear
Lyre or sonnet,
All my life's buried here,
Heap earth upon it.

Comfort
(Anon)

When your heart is sad and lonely,
And your friends seem far away,
Turn to Him who is all holy,
And He'll drive your cares away.

When a dear one seems far from you,
When for friendship true you long,
Confide in Him who is all true,
And He'll right your every wrong.
Jesus' heart is your true refuge,
To Him you can always flee,
Even when your hopes are sinking
He will then a true friend be.

He will soothe your lonely spirit,
He will love and bless and say,
'Come to me and I will comfort
You, today and every day.'

PRAYERS

Every Day I Need You Lord
(Prayer of St Gertrude)

Every day I need you Lord
But this day especially,
I need some extra strength
To face whatever is to be.

This day more than any day
I need to feel you near,
To fortify my courage
And overcome my fear.

By myself I cannot meet
The challenge of the hour,
There are times when humans help
But we need a higher power

To assist us bear what must be borne.
And so dear Lord, I pray –
Hold on to my trembling hand
And be near me today.
Amen.

We Seem to Give Them Back to You
(Bishop Charles Henry Brent)

We seem to give the back to you, O God who gave them to us.
Yet as you did not lose them in giving,
So do we not lose them by their return.
Not as the world gives, give you O lover of souls.
What you give, you take not away,
For what is yours is ours also if we are yours.
And death is only a horizon,
And a horizon is nothing save the limit of our sight.
Lift us up, strong Son of God that we may see further;
Cleanse our eyes that we may see more clearly;
Draw us closer to yourself
That we may know ourselves to be nearer
to our loved ones who are with you.
And while you prepare a place for us, prepare us also for that
happy place,
That where you are we may also be for evermore.

Our Work Is Done
(St John Henry Newman)

O Lord support us all the day long of this troublous life, until the
shadows lengthen, and the evening comes, and the busy world
is hushed, the fever of life is over, and our work is done. Then,
Lord, in your mercy, grant us safe lodging, a holy rest, and peace at
the last. Through Jesus Christ our Lord. Amen.

From the Roman Ritual

In the name of God the almighty Father who created you,
in the name of Jesus Christ, Son of the living God, who suffered
for you,
in the name of the Holy Spirit, who was poured out upon you,
go forth, faithful Christian.
May you live in peace this day,
may your home be with God in Zion,
with Mary the virgin Mother of God,
with Joseph, and all the angels and saints.

Prayer of Commendation
(from the *Order of Christian Funerals*)

Into your hands, Father of mercies,
we commend our brother/sister
in the sure and certain hope
that, together with all who have died in Christ,
he/she will rise with him on the last day.
Merciful Lord,
turn towards us and listen to our prayers:
open the gates of paradise to your servant
and help us who remain
to comfort one another with assurances of faith,
until we all meet in Christ
and are with you and with our brother/sister for ever.
Amen.

BIBLIOGRAPHY

D'Arcy, Brian, *A Little Bit of Healing*, Dublin: The Columba Press, 2010.

McKeown, Laurence, *Threads,* Ennistymon: Salmon Poetry, 2018.

Magee, Brian CM (Editor), *Funeral Rites & Readings,* Dublin: Veritas Publications, 1995.

O'Donohue, John, *Anam Chara: Spiritual Wisdom from the Celtic World,* London: Bantam Books, 1997.

O'Donohue, John, *Benedictus, A Book of Blessings*, London: Bantam Books, 2007.

Owen, David M., *Living Through Bereavement (With the help of Christian thought and prayer)*, London: SPCK, 2008.

A Celebration of Life (When a Loved One Dies), Dundalk: Redemptorist Communications, 2015.

Parkes, Colin Murray, *Bereavement: Studies of Grief in Adult Life,* London: Penguin, 1975.

Spark, Muriel, *The Only Problem,* Edinburgh: Polygon, 2018.

Worden, William J., *Grief Counselling and Grief Therapy*, Abingdon: Routledge 1993.

Order of Christian Funerals (Approved for use in the Dioceses of Ireland), Dublin: Veritas Publications 1991.

A Pocket Ritual, Southend-on-Sea: McCrimmon Publishing Co. Ltd, 1997.